Gift Aid Non fiction
£

0 031140 052635

Δ   33/24   TR1   £5

KU-114-042

THE
GRESLEY PACIFICS
OF THE
L. N. E. R.

by

C E C I L J. A L L E N
M.Inst.T., A.I.Loco.E.

LONDON:

Ian Allan Ltd

First Published *1950*

Contents

Foreword

There could have been few tasks more wholly congenial than the writing of this book.   If in all my forty years and more of writing on locomotive practice and performance I could have been accused of departing from strict impartiality to the extent of having a "favourite" locomotive class, I cannot help thinking that the choice would have fallen on the Gresley Pacifics of the L.N.E.R.   And even to-day, the sight of a sleek and purposeful "A4" at the head of the train in which I am about to travel still arouses more pleasurable reactions than those excited by most of the ultra-modern rivals of these famous machines.

However, there are some very substantial grounds for such a preference.   All the principal speed records in Great Britain have been made by Gresley's streamlined "A4s"—a maximum speed of 126 m.p.h., 43 miles right off at an average of 100 m.p.h., and an ability, shown by no other class of locomotive in Great Britain, to run at 100 m.p.h. and over even on level track.   At the other end of the scale, Gresley Pacifics have hauled the heaviest express passenger trains ever known in this country, up to 850 tons in gross weight.   Between speed and weight, what other British locomotive type has been expected to keep time with a train like the 550-ton "Flying Scotsman" on a mile-a-minute schedule over such gradients as those between Grantham and King's Cross?

To a lover of the Gresley Pacifics, it is no small encouragement to note how these engines still can hold their own against competitors of later design.   It was significant indeed that in the 1948 Locomotive Exchange the engines chosen to represent the Eastern Region in the express passenger class were none of the many variations of the Gresley design evolved by his successors, but "A4s"—undiluted Gresley.   The results were a Gresley triumph indeed, for in coal and water consumption proportioned to power output the "A4" engines beat all comers with the lowest figures of any.   Even the Western

Region "King," specially fitted with high temperature super-heating equipment, and burning its own Welsh coal over its own main line to the West, could not get down to the "A4" coal and water consumption when the "A4" was burning Yorkshire coal on the Eastern Region main line to Leeds.

It is true that in the trials *Mallard* and *Seagull* both had heating troubles with that susceptible middle big-end. Almost a whole chapter of this book is devoted to a discussion of this most debatable of all the characteristic details of Gresley practice embodied in his Pacifics—the conjugated motion for the inside cylinder, with its tendency to over-run the middle valve. Yet, when these engines have been properly maintained, this feature has given little trouble, and it would be hard to find a parallel for some of the feats of endurance, as shown in continuous running on extremely hard assignments, for which Gresley Pacifics have been responsible. As yet there is little evidence that the many variations of the Gresley Pacific design that have been made since his death have produced engines that are either more reliable or more economical.

These later developments form no part of the subject matter indicated by the title of this book, and beyond the rebuilding of the original No. 4470, *Great Northern*, a Gresley engine, I have made no attempt to deal with them. But the Gresley Pacifics themselves have been covered in the fullest manner possible, and I trust that no detail of importance in their distinguished history has been omitted, not even the complexities of three renumberings of the series, nor the curious jugglery with nameplates that has taken place between one engine and another. Some of the thrills attending the various high speed trials may be familiar to readers from articles that I have written on the subject previously, but the stories can bear re-telling, and there are many readers, I think, who will be glad to have them in this collated form.

Twenty-eight years have elapsed since the never-to-be-forgotten day when I had my first sight of G.N.R. No. 1470, standing opposite the main booking-hall door at King's Cross, the cynosure of all eyes. No engines could be more familiar to me than these; in many years of travelling between London and Tees-side, often to and fro every week, and interspersed at regular intervals with longer journeys to Edinburgh, Glasgow and Aberdeen, there must be few, if any, of the 114 engines that I have not ridden behind at one time or another. And rare indeed, up to the Second World War, have been the occasions when a run with a Gresley Pacific has not been worth recording.

Yes, in those halcyon years from 1932 to 1939 it was my privilege to see and to record Gresley Pacific performance of a quality possibly equalled elsewhere at times, but certainly never excelled. It was my even greater privilege to know the designer himself—no remote Olympian, but a man readily approachable, genial and friendly, especially to anyone who took an interest in and wrote appreciatively of the work of his engines. Eight years have passed since his death, but the memory of him remains green and long will continue to do so. And the Gresley Pacifics, still in 1950 earning their laurels, are destined to occupy for all time one of the most prominent places in the roll of fame of British locomotive history.

In conclusion, I have to express my warm thanks to my friends Mr. Arthur F. Cook, M.A., and Mr. R. A. H. Weight for their valuable help in ensuring that this book shall be an accurate presentation of a fascinating subject.

Hatch End,
March, 1950.   CECIL J. ALLEN.

1

The Emergence of "Great Northern"

One afternoon in the spring of 1922, when returning from my usual round of weekly travel to Barnet, where I then lived, I was making my way to the "Local" station at King's Cross by way of the principal departure platform at the terminus—then No. 1—when my progress was suddenly arrested. In those days the island platform on the departure side of the main station had not been built, and the space between the present Nos. 6 and 10 platforms was occupied by sidings and a short loading dock for horses, carriages and motors at the inner end.

On this never-to-be-forgotten day a new articulated sleeping car was standing alongside the loading dock, and beyond that —shining, stately and strikingly impressive—the most massive locomotive that I had ever set eyes on in Great Britain until then. It was No. 1470 *Great Northern*, Gresley's first Pacific, brought to London to be exhibited to the directors of his company, the Great Northern Railway. But the engine was destined to have a great many other admirers that day; for myself, my baggage was deposited on the platform for a considerable time while I endeavoured to take in every feature of this new monster of the rails, and as a result I reached home well after my "advertised time"!

For months previously rumours had been going the rounds as to what Gresley was "doing" at Doncaster. The successful running of his Moguls, first introduced in 1912 and culminating in the "K3" 3-cylinder design of 1920, prompted the idea that the new engine would be a 2-6-2; actually a 2-6-2 design had been considered seriously. The "K3" class engines had shown themselves capable of speeds well in excess of 70 m.p.h., notwithstanding driving wheels of no more than 5 ft. 8 in. diameter, and with the first-class maintenance of Great Northern track their pony trucks had given no trouble at speed. As events proved, however, we were to wait another fourteen years, until 1936, for the materialisation of the first Gresley main line 2-6-2; and the new Great Northern engine of 1922 proved to be a Pacific. It was not the first Pacific to run in Great Britain, of course, for G. J. Churchward of the Great Western Railway had preceded Gresley by fourteen years with *The Great Bear* of 1908. But whereas Churchward, probably for the only time in his brilliant career, built a locomotive which could not be regarded as a success, which was never multiplied, and which eventually was converted to a 4-6-0, Gresley with No. 1470 initiated a series of locomotives which more than any other of his designs has qualified him to take a place among the immortals of British locomotive history.

The late Sir Nigel Gresley in every sense of the word was a "big" man. The bigness of his physical frame matched the breadth of his vision. Although, as we shall see later, he could be a traditionalist when he chose, possibly even to the disadvantage of his engines, in general he was receptive to all ideas, from wherever they might come, and he was never small-minded enough to consider that his reputation might suffer if he were to acknowledge the source of any inspiration. Whether as Chief Mechanical Engineer of the Great Northern Railway, or, later, of the London & North Eastern Railway, he had the great advantage of being master in his own house, and of having a free hand in the development of his ideas, without any interference from operating officers whose notions as to what was required might be cast in a less heroic mould.

The bigness of the Gresley mind equally was reflected in the bigness of his locomotives. More than any other British locomotive engineer he specialised in a "big engine" policy; instead of letting his locomotives catch up on events, he built for the future, as with No. 1470, which he proclaimed would be adequate for the haulage of 600-ton trains at a time when a 400-ton load on the Great Northern main line was regarded as very heavy indeed. Bit by bit, as new Pacifics were added to the London & North Eastern stock, and the "A3" and "A4" classes later joined the original "A1s," Gresley provided the London & North Eastern Railway with a stud of powerful locomotives which had ample reserve to meet every possible

THE
ORIGINAL
"A1s"

(Above) No. 1471 in Great Northern livery, before being named.

[W. J. Reynolds

(Left) No.1471 working hard past Wood Green with the 20-coach test train of September, 1922. The engine carries an indicator shelter round the smokebox

[H. Gordon Tidey

(Above)

WITH ORIGINAL CHIMNEY AND CAB —"A1" No. 4478 *Hermit* heads the 5.45 p.m. King's Cross— Leeds and Bradford express past Ganwick, Middlesex, in 1928.

[*F. R. Hebron*

(Left)

THE 1925 EXCHANGE —"A1" No. 4474, then unnamed, enters Paddington with the G.W.R. up "Cornish Riviera Express" on April 30th.

FIRST OF THE L.N.E.R. "A1s" was No. 4472 *Flying Scotsman*, which for a long time was unique with L.N.E.R. crest on the cabside and brass beadings to the splashers.

[W. J. Reynolds

THE FIRST EXPERIMENT—"A1" No. 4477 *Gay Crusader* in 1926 after modification to valves and valve gear.

[P. Ransome-Wallis

THE FIRST "A3"—Rebuilt No. 4480 *Enterprise* on an up slow train at Retford.

[F. R. Hebron

"A1s" AT WORK—A down Scotch express passing New Southgate in 1925. No. 2550 (unnamed) in charge. No. 2550 was one of the second L.N.E.R. batch, built with the cut-down boiler mountings now standard.

extreme of load or weather without needing pilot assistance, or, on the other hand, losing time.

Another feature of Gresley's work as a designer is worth emphasis. When he had designed and built a new locomotive class, the engines went straight out on to the road and began to earn dividends from the word "go." There was no wearisome succession of revisits to "Plant" for the adjustment of this, that or the other, or for boiler modifications, or for any other reason. Each design had been thought out with the utmost thoroughness in the drawing office, and with his engines most subsequent alterations that must have made certain other new British locomotive classes very costly to their owners have been unnecessary. So it was with No. 1470 and her successors, and in one respect only, as was to be proved in striking fashion three years later, did Gresley allow conservatism to enter into his design in a way which affected, not the ability of the engines to pull, but the efficiency or the reverse with which they used their fuel.

Throughout its independent history, from 1850 to 1922, the Great Northern Railway was fortunate in having no more than four Locomotive Superintendents—Archibald Sturrock, Patrick Stirling, H. A. Ivatt and H. N. Gresley—so that there was a continuity in locomotive design policy of a rarity seen elsewhere only on the Great Western Railway. In the principal Great Northern express locomotive designs, therefore, there was a logical development from Stirling's 8 ft. $1\frac{1}{2}$ in. 4-2-2 of 1870 to Ivatt's large-boilered 4-4-2 of 1902 and finally to Gresley's 4-6-2 of 1922.

There was one feature of design, however, in which both Ivatt and Gresley differed radically from Stirling. The last named was inclined to over-cylinder his engines, particularly his last series of 4-2-2s, in which he followed the dubious course of trying to obtain increased tractive power merely by increasing cylinder dimensions, without any increase in the capacity of his boiler to raise steam. In the last of these, Nos. 1003 to 1008 inclusive, the diameter and stroke of the cylinders were increased to no less than $19\frac{1}{2}$ in. and 28 in. respectively; by contrast, the diminutive 4 ft. diameter boiler which had to supply them with steam contained no more than 1,031 sq. ft. of heating surface and 20 sq. ft. of firegrate area, though the grate was certainly bigger than the 17·6 sq. ft. of the original Stirling 8-footers.

In the first Ivatt large-boilered Atlantics the change in these proportions was revolutionary indeed, for cylinders of 18¾ in. diameter and 24in. stroke were mated to a 5 ft. 6 in. diameter boiler providing no less than 2,500 sq. ft. of heating surface and 31 sq. ft. of grate. Ivatt's *dictum* has often been quoted that the measure of a locomotive's success is its "ability to boil water," and this was exemplified to a remarkable degree in Atlantic No. 251. That is to say, whereas Stirling's No. 1003 had 106 sq. ft. of heating surface and 2·07 sq. ft. of fire-grate area to every cubic foot of cylinder volume, in No. 251 these proportions had changed to 326 to 1 and 4·00 to 1 respectively.

Gresley's first Pacific took a position midway between these two extremes. With three 20 in. × 26 in. cylinders, 3,455 sq. ft. of heating surface (including superheater) and 41·25 sq. ft. of firegrate, the proportion of heating surface to cylinder volume had come down again to 165 sq. ft. to 1 cub. ft., and firegrate area to cylinder volume was now a shade less than 2·00 sq. ft. to 1 cub. ft. Where the Pacific scored heavily over both its predecessors, however, was in the matter of adhesion. The driving axle of the Stirling 8-footer carried 19 tons of the engine's weight; in No. 251 the adhesion weight went up to 36 tons; in No. 1470 the weight available for adhesion had risen to 60 tons. The Stirling 8-footers, in the days of light non-corridor stock, largely six-wheelers, had been just about equal to their work, with little reserve; the Ivatt Atlantics, after superheating, could do splendidly, even with heavy trains, in every respect other than starting up steep grades; the Gresley Pacifics, on their introduction, were far ahead of all the traffic demands of that time.

2

The "A1" Pacifics

With the foregoing chapter by way of introduction, we come now to a more detailed examination of the first Gresley Pacific design. While the engine embodied various features which were to be expected, from the practice already developed by Gresley, other details were new to the G.N.R. Of the expected features, the use of three cylinders, with the Gresley derived motion for the inside cylinder, was, of course, one. Another was the wide type of firebox, which had proved so successful with the Ivatt Atlantics; and the engine-crews had become so accustomed to firing the square type of grate of the latter, rather than the long narrow grate in general use elsewhere, that no undue difficulty in firing need be foreseen in the increase of firegrate area from 30·9 to 41·25 sq. ft.

But the chief novelty was the use of a tapered boiler barrel. The "K3" Moguls had shown that a parallel boiler up to 6 ft. diameter could be accommodated within the confines of the British loading gauge; in No. 1470 it was seen that Gresley, starting with a diameter of 5 ft. 9 in. at the smokebox end, had tapered the barrel out to no less a diameter than 6 ft. 5 in. at the firebox end. The crown-plate of the firebox, on the other hand, tapered downwards towards the cab, so providing the maximum cross-sectional area immediately adjacent to the barrel, where the heat values are greatest. Also the firebox was arranged to taper inwards on both sides towards the cab, thus giving an unusually fine look-out with a boiler of such large size. While these tapered fireboxes were standard G.W.R. Belpaire practice, Gresley was the first to apply the same principle to a round-topped firebox. The boiler was pitched with its centre-line 9 ft. 4 in. above rail level.

Gresley was careful to avoid excessive length in his boiler-tubes, and therefore mounted the smokebox of the engine with its centre-line well in rear of the bogie centre-line. The distance between tubeplates was further reduced, by the projection of the firebox for a short distance into the barrel, to an actual figure of 19 ft.; this also had the effect of increasing the firebox heating surface and providing the firebox with a small additional area to serve as a combustion chamber, and so to assist in complete combustion of the fuel. Some complicated flanging work was needed at Doncaster in shaping both the inner and outer fireboxes and the throat-plate.

At the front end, the lay-out of so large an engine within the confines of the British loading gauge called for most careful planning, and in some respects the engine suffered from its size. In his multi-cylinder engines Gresley would go to considerable lengths in order to secure undivided drive—that is, to drive with all three cylinders on the same axle. He had a strong objection to driving on a leading coupled axle, as this made it impossible to give the latter the lateral play that he thought essential, and he was influenced also by his individualistic ideas on balancing, which are discussed in Chapter 6. To obtain undivided drive on No. 1470, it was necessary to raise the middle cylinder, and to incline it sharply at an angle of 1 in 8, so that the leading coupled axle might be cleared.

In this location Gresley's derived motion for the inside cylinder played a useful part. By eliminating the crosshead connection of an independent valve-motion for the inside cylinder, the designer could bring his inside crosshead down close enough to the leading axle to keep the inclined cylinder well clear of the base of the smokebox; and in any event there would not have been room enough to fit a Walschaerts gear to a cylinder inclined at such an angle. But there was plenty of space available in which to mount the 2-to-1 levers of the derived motion across the front of the engine, ahead of the three cylinders. A disadvantage of mounting the three cylinders in line, however, was that it limited the size of the piston-valves to 8 in. diameter—a feature that evoked some criticism at the time, as these valves were required to supply 20 in. cylinders, and it was held that so small a diameter might restrict the steam flow.

The conservatism to which reference has been made previously was seen in the boiler pressure and the valve-setting. With the former, notwithstanding the known and obvious success of Churchward's 225 lb. per sq. in., on the Great

Western, Gresley decided to stick to 180 lb., though he would find some justification, of course, in the reduced costs of maintaining boilers at the lower pressure. As to the valve-setting, $1\frac{1}{4}$ in. lap, $\frac{1}{4}$ in. exhaust clearance, $\frac{3}{16}$ in. lead, and a maximum valve-travel of $4\frac{9}{16}$ in. at 65 per cent. cut-off, meant that most of the work of the engine necessarily would be done with a relatively long cut-off and the regulator no more than partially open.

The limitation of maximum cut-off to 65 per cent. was for a reason revealed by Mr. B. Spencer in his paper "The Development of the L.N.E.R. Locomotive Design, 1923-1941," read to the Institution of Locomotive Engineers on March 19th, 1947. When the first "K3" 2-6-0, No. 1000, was being tested on express passenger trains, it was found that the cover of the centre piston-valve chest had been damaged by the crosshead spindle of the centre valve. Apparently the latter had over-run—i.e., its travel had increased beyond the theoretical maximum—by the engine having been put into the full 75 per cent. cut-off when coasting with the regulator shut. The "whip" under strain of the long 2-to-1 lever, or of the stay supporting its fulcrum, or both, had been largely responsible. It was discovered, too, that at high speeds, with the regulator full open, the middle cylinder was doing more than its proper one-third share of the work. At that time the "K3" had $6\frac{3}{8}$ in. valve-travel at 75 per cent. cut-off, with $1\frac{1}{2}$ in. lap, $\frac{1}{8}$ in. exhaust clearance and $\frac{1}{8}$ in. lead.

For these reasons the Pacific cut-off limitation to a maximum of 65 per cent. was decided on, reducing the maximum valve-travel by about 1 in. In one respect at least the Gresley Pacifics have suffered from this restraint, because it has made them somewhat deficient in tractive effort when the maximum effort is needed, as when getting away with a heavy train from a sharply curved platform; the deficiency is more pronounced, also, with a three-cylinder than with a two-cylinder or four-cylinder engine. Many readers no doubt have shared my experience in seeing one of these engines in considerable difficulties when starting weighty trains out of Newcastle or northwards out of York. At one time, rear-end assistance out of Newcastle became a regular procedure with the principal East Coast trains.

The light and graceful details of the rods and motion of
No. 1470 were due to the use of heat-treated nickel-chrome
steel for these parts. Both connecting and coupling-rods
were milled out to form an I-section, and the deep web of the
connecting-rod was no more than $\frac{5}{16}$ in. thick. This lightening
of weight was made possible by the tensile strength of the heat-
treated alloy being some 50 per cent. greater than that of
ordinary mild steel, and has been helpful in reducing hammer-
blow and other stresses set up by the unbalanced forces of the
reciprocating motion. Another beneficial effect has been to
assist the extremely smooth riding of these engines, in which
also the careful design of the springing has been of great value.

For the Great Northern Railway the cab fitted by Gresley to
his Pacific was an entirely new departure, with its high arched
roof and two windows in either side. Its level floor and
general spaciousness made it an immeasurable advance on the
cabs of the Ivatt Atlantics, and to drivers and firemen the
exchange of the violent antics of the latter on the road for the
smooth and easy travel of the bigger machines must have been
a most welcome improvement. The pull-out type of regulator
so long standard on the G.N.R. was retained, but with
operating handles on both sides of the cab; a distinctive
Gresley feature of the cab equipment was the vertical reversing
column, working in conjunction with a vacuum-operated
clutch on the reversing shaft. A very clear type of cut-off
percentage indicator, working vertically on the back of the
firebox, coupled with the provision of a steam-chest pressure
gauge, enabled the driver of a Pacific to follow the working of
both his regulator and valve-motion with a precision not
possible before on the G.N.R., or, for that matter, on any
other British railway.

A novelty for the Great Northern Railway was the first use
of an 8-wheel tender. Unlike the double bogie tenders of the
London & South Western, Caledonian and Glasgow & South
Western Railways, and the tender built by Churchward for
The Great Bear, however, the tender of No. 1470 was carried
on four rigid axles. At the time this arrangement caused some
surprise, but it has proved perfectly successful in practice, and
has been the standard for all L.N.E.R. Pacifics since. The
first Pacific tenders had spoked wheels, but at a later date the

solid disc type of wheel was introduced, and subsequently became standard practice. Incidentally, the use of an 8-wheel in place of a 6-wheel tender added to the problem of length which had been set by the change from the 4-4-2 to the 4-6-2 wheel arrangement; the increase was from an engine and tender wheelbase of 48 ft. 5¾ in. and an overall length of 57 ft. 10¼ in., with the Atlantic, to 60 ft. 10 in. and 70 ft. 5 in. respectively with the Pacific, and the latter could not be turned on anything less than a 65 ft. turntable.

At the start two of the new Pacifics were built: No. 1470 appeared in April, 1922, and No. 1471 followed three months later, No. 1471 at first without name. Two months after the latter's emergence from Doncaster Works a test run was arranged from King's Cross to Grantham and back to substantiate Gresley's contention that the new engines would find no difficulty in handling 600-ton trains. The train actually made up consisted of 20 vehicles, and weighed 610 tons. It took 7½ minutes to get through Finsbury Park, 24 minutes to Potter's Bar, 30 minutes to Hatfield and 46 minutes to Hitchin, but the next 27 miles to Huntingdon were run in 23 minutes, and Peterborough was cleared in 86 minutes. The climb of 23·7 miles from Peterborough to Stoke was accomplished in exactly half-an-hour, with an average speed of 45 m.p.h. up the final 1 in 178, and Grantham, 105·5 miles, was reached in 122 minutes from London. In the light of Gresley Pacific performances in later years this run, though excellent, would excite no special comment, of course; but back in 1922 it was an eye-opener indeed.

On the strength of the performances of Nos. 1470 and 1471, ten more Pacifics were put on order in the same year, but when the first of this batch, No. 1472 *Flying Scotsman*, appeared in January, 1923, there was no longer any Great Northern Railway; the G.N.R. had become merged in the London & North Eastern Railway. The ten new Pacifics were all completed during 1923, and were numbered 1472 to 1481 inclusive; their names were as set out in Appendix I, which gives the numbers and names borne by all the Gresley Pacifics at the various stages of their history.

In the early summer of 1923 I was permitted to ride on the footplate of No. 1473 *Solario* from Doncaster to King's Cross, and the handling of the engine furnishes a striking contrast to the way in which they have been worked in later years; nothing could illustrate more clearly the effect of a valve-gear laid out with the traditional short lap and short valve-travel of byegone days. The train was the 10 a.m. from Leeds to London, then due to leave Doncaster at 10.51 a.m., and with stops at Retford, Grantham and Peterborough to be into King's Cross by 1.55 p.m. With a normal formation of 13 coaches from Doncaster and 14 from Grantham, or about 440 tons and 475-480 tons over each stage, it was regarded by the enginemen as one of the hardest turns of the day.

There was no question as to the ability of *Solario* to keep time. Despite a little loss of time at the start through brakes dragging on, we ran the 17·4 miles to Retford in 21 min. 15 sec., start to stop, with a top speed of 70½ m.p.h. at Scrooby troughs; then we attained 48 m.p.h. on the climb from Retford to Markham, reached 80½ m.p.h. by Crow Park, and after crossing the wide level of the Trent Valley were still doing 68 at Newark, but only to be stopped dead by adverse signals at a small box called Balderton. The 21·6 miles from Retford to Balderton took 23 min. 25 sec. start to stop, and the 11·7 uphill miles from there to Grantham 16 min. 30 sec.; net time from Retford to Grantham was about 36 minutes for the 33·1 miles, as against a booking of 38 minutes.

From Grantham, now with the full 480 tons, we did finely to climb the 5·4 miles at 1 in 200 to Stoke in 9 min. 10 sec. from the start; then came a long spell of very fast running, with a maximum of 82 m.p.h., which brought us into Peterborough in 30 min. 25 sec. for the 29·1 miles, schedule 33 minutes. Out of Peterborough the engine lost 1 min. 20 sec. to Huntingdon—21 min. 20 sec. for the very sharply-timed 17·5 miles—but easily recouped the loss, more especially after Hitchin, where we topped the lengthy 1 in 200 to Stevenage at 48 m.p.h., and finished with a rousing 18 min. 5 sec. for the final 17·7 miles from Hatfield into King's Cross, including 77½ m.p.h. through Wood Green. This made a total of 81 min. 25 sec. for the 76·4 miles from Peterborough, against 84 minutes scheduled. In all, the engine had gained about 7 minutes.

But how was this done? For the major part of the journey

the cut-off was fixed at 45 per cent.   On the easy and downhill stretches, the regulator was about one-half open; up the banks three-quarters open and 50 per cent., or four-fifths and 45 per cent., were the normal settings.   Starts, of course, were on the full permissible 65 per cent. cut-off.   Never once did I see the regulator full open.   The pressure in the boiler varied a good deal.   In climbing from Retford to Markham it rose from 160 to 170 lb.;   by Newark it had dropped to 140 lb.;   for most of the journey about 160 to 170 lb. was the figure.   By the look of the tender on arrival, we had burned perhaps $3\frac{1}{4}$ tons on the 156 mile run, which would work out at nearly 47 lb. per mile; normally the original Gresley Pacifics could be reckoned on as consuming an average of round about 50 lb. to the mile, on all their duties.   Two years were to pass before the extravagance of such a coal consumption was to be made apparent; meantime the engines were able to handle any load, and as thoroughly reliable machines were giving every satisfaction.

It is worth recording that during the summer of 1923 one of the Raven Pacifics of the North Eastern Railway, No. 2400 *City of Newcastle*, was tried against the Gresley Pacifics between King's Cross and Doncaster.   There had been a certain amount of competition between Raven and Gresley as to which of the two designs would take the road first, but in this Gresley had won by a handsome margin.   North Eastern locomotive enthusiasts have sometimes felt aggrieved that of the two the Gresley design won in the end, but this was undoubtedly a matter of merit and not of favouritism.

In his book "The Locomotives of Sir Nigel Gresley," Mr. O. S. Nock has revealed that on trains like the 10.51 a.m. from Doncaster to London, on which I have just described a run of complete competence with the Gresley Pacific *Solario*, the North Eastern Pacific found difficulty in keeping time; as with the former, the latter's average cut-off was 40 per cent., and boiler pressure averaged 165 lb., but the coal consumption was 50 lb. to the mile, and *City of Newcastle* suffered from heating troubles as well.   The North Eastern boiler was one of the weaknesses of the Raven engine, and although another of the same series was tried with a Gresley Pacific boiler, no real success was obtained with any of the five North Eastern "A2" Pacifics, and their early scrapping was a matter of no surprise. Moreover, it was not until after the events related in the next chapter that even the Gresley Pacifics really entered into their own.

It was well on in 1923 before the last of Gresley's initial batch of "A1" Pacifics, No. 1481 *St. Simon*, appeared from Doncaster Works. The loading gauges of the northern constituents of the L.N.E.R. group, and in particular of what had been the North British Railway, were not so generous as that of the Great Northern, and it was realised that if the Pacifics were to work through to Edinburgh, clearances north of the Border were too scanty for them to pass in comfort. *St. Simon* therefore emerged in a cut-down form, with a maximum height of 13 ft. 1 in. above rail instead of the previous 13 ft. 4 in. This affected the chimney, which was shortened and reduced in diameter, and the high arched roof of the cab had to be reduced similarly, with a perceptible change in the appearance of the engine. All subsequent "A1" Pacifics appeared in the same form as *St. Simon*, and the previous eleven engines were cut down correspondingly.

By 1924 the first all-L.N.E.R. system of engine numbering had been settled, with 3,000 added to the Great Northern numbers, so that Pacifics Nos. 1470 to 1481 now became Nos. 4470 to 4481 inclusive. Moreover, the success of the design was by now so firmly established that in the same year the building of forty more "A1" Pacifics was decided on, twenty by Doncaster Works and the remaining twenty by the North British Locomotive Company in Glasgow, the former numbered from 2543 to 2562 and the latter from 2563 to 2582. All the Scottish-built series were turned out during 1924, but Nos. 2555 to 2562 appeared from Doncaster in 1925.

Nos. 2563 to 2582 were fitted with the Westinghouse brake, as they were intended for the North Eastern Area, on which air-brakes until then had been standard. Before 1924 was out the first Scottish-built Pacific, No. 2563, *William Whitelaw*, had made its way as far north as Aberdeen, and in the following year the first Pacific trials were made between Marylebone and Manchester with No. 4473 *Solario*, foreshadowing the wide range of action that these engines eventually would enjoy.

3

Pacific versus "Castle"

At the beginning of 1923, with the advent of the grouping, Gresley was chosen by the Directors of the London & North Eastern Railway to be Chief Mechanical Engineer of the new system, and the continuity of his Doncaster practice thus became assured. As previously mentioned, however, Gresley was a man with great breadth of vision, and this was evident from the way in which his locomotive building, in the early years of his L.N.E.R. *régime*, was not confined to Great Northern types alone, but included further batches of successful classes from other railways brought into the L.N.E.R. group, such as the Great Central "Director" 4-4-0s and "A5" 4-6-2 tanks of Robinson's design, and the Holden "B12" 4-6-0s and Hill "N7" 0-6-2 tanks of the Great Eastern. But for heavy express passenger work the Gresley Pacific design had no serious rival, and remained unaffected by the change in railway ownership.

One immediate result of the grouping was greatly to intensify the competitive nature of railway advertising in Great Britain. Each of the four new main line systems now could afford to spend a good deal more on publicity than had been possible with most of the individual railways previously, and the newly-established publicity departments lost no time in exploiting these possibilities. An urge arose to lay claim to records in every realm of railway equipment and operation— the biggest, the fastest, and so on—and all kinds of figures and statistics came under scrutiny in the interests of prestige and publicity. Among these rivalries, possession of the most powerful locomotive was thought to be a strong advertising point, and this particular competition was destined to have some very startling results.

In the year 1924, to mark the recovery from the effects of the First World War, the British Empire Exhibition was opened at Wembley. As one of the most spectacular railway exhibits in the Palace of Engineering, the London & North Eastern Railway installed on its stand "A1" Pacific No. 4472 *Flying Scotsman*, superbly finished with various embellishments in brass, polished steel and colour not possessed by other engines of the same type. Not to be outdone, the Great Western Railway brought to its immediately adjacent stand No. 4073 *Caerphilly Castle*, first of a new series of enlarged "Star" class 4-6-0s that had emerged from Swindon in the previous year: the "Castle" design thus was one year younger than the Gresley Pacific.

At first glance the Great Western engine, with its lower-pitched boiler, of much smaller diameter at the smokebox end, shorter wheelbase and length overall, and six-wheel as against eight-wheel tender, seemed much the less imposing of the two engines. But visitors to the stands were intrigued by the notice which the G.W.R. exhibited in a prominent position in front of their engine, claiming it to be " the most powerful express passenger locomotive in Great Britain." On the face of it the claim seemed absurd, but on the basis of the tractive force formula it was, of course, justified. For *Caerphilly Castle*, with a working pressure of 225 lb. per sq. in., could put out a tractive effort of 31,625 lb. (at the usual 85 per cent. of the boiler pressure), while the Pacific, though with the larger cylinder volume of the two engines, was tied down by Gresley's conservatism in boiler pressure to a maximum of 29,835 lb.

But could the "Castle" boiler produce steam at the rate necessary to make the Great Western claim effective? This was the question which was to be answered in the following year, and with such emphasis as eventually to effect a radical change in the Gresley Pacific design. For the outcome of the Wembley Exhibition was a challenge—in precisely what terms it was made or from what precise quarter it came has never been revealed—by the London & North Eastern Railway to the Great Western Railway to prove which company really was entitled to claim "the most powerful engine." So there came about the famous exchange of locomotives between the two companies, which took place towards the end of April, 1925.

A full account of what transpired is included, with detailed logs of some of the most outstanding performances, in my recent book "The Locomotive Exchanges, 1870-1948*," but this review of the Gresley Pacifics and their history would be incomplete without brief reference to one of the most exciting fortnights in British locomotive history. For however the owners of the two engines may have attempted to represent the trials as nothing more than a friendly exchange of information, the public, and railway enthusiasts in particular, regarded it as a sporting event of the first magnitude; the test routes were lined with excited spectators, and great crowds watched the starts and finishes of the test runs, especially at the London terminals.

From the L.N.E.R. there went over to the G.W.R. No. 4474 *Victor Wild*, in charge of Driver Pibworth and Fireman Birkwood, and the engine could not have had a more competent crew. As with the 1948 exchanges, the tests covered a fortnight, one week for learning the road and the next week with the stiffest test the Great Western could produce—the 10.30 a.m. down "Cornish Riviera Limited" non-stop from Paddington to Plymouth one day, and the corresponding up express on the next, a round three times repeated from Monday to Saturday. To master a tricky road like the Western, with its alluring stretches of level and then its sudden and formidable obstacles, such as the climb to Whiteball in Somerset and finally the fearsome gradients west of Newton Abbot, is something that no driver could possibly do in no more than a week of preliminary running, and in such conditions the exactitude with which Pibworth succeeded in maintaining his point-to-point times was a masterly feat indeed. No late arrivals in either direction were booked against him in either direction of the test week proper.

His fireman had an even more difficult task. Firing the 41 sq. ft. of a Pacific firegrate with soft Welsh coking steam coal, which had been loaded on the tender in very large lumps, was a different proposition entirely from using the normal hard Yorkshire coal, and required a totally different technique, but with friendly assistance from the Great Western pilotman, Birkwood was able to adapt his methods with such skill as to bring No. 4474's coal consumption on the three eastbound journeys down from 50·9 lb. per mile on the first trip to

*Published by Ian Allan, Ltd. (1949).

45·2 lb. on the second and 40·4 lb. on the third. On the far harder westbound workings the consumptions were 50·0, 48·8 and 52·4 lb. per mile, the increase on the third run being due to a very high wind on that day which caught the train broadside most of the way from Paddington to Taunton.

The down "Limited" was booked through Westbury, 95·6 miles from Paddington, in 97½ minutes, with a load of just under 500 tare tons (530 tons gross); slipping two coaches there and two more at Taunton, the train had fallen to 361 tare tons in weight from Taunton, which meant 385 gross tons to get over Whiteball summit; Exeter, 173·7 miles, had to be passed in 179 minutes; and after the loss of a third slip portion, the load remaining to be worked up the 1 in 40 to Dainton and the 1 in 50 of Rattery bank was 292 tons tare and 310 tons gross. On the run which I made behind *Victor Wild*, we lost nearly 3 minutes to Westbury because of the wind (100 min. 20 sec. to this point), but by fine running from there passed Taunton, 142·9 miles, a minute early in 147 min. exactly; there was another loss of nearly 2 minutes to Exeter, but notwithstanding permanent way checks on either side of Newton Abbot and on the approach to Plymouth, *Victor Wild* stopped triumphantly at North Road in 246 min. 45 sec. from Paddington, 15 seconds ahead of time.

But the Pacific's competitor on Great Western metals, No. 4074 *Caldicot Castle*, was in charge of the redoubtable Edward Rowe, a driver of sporting temperament who, given the road, worried little about any restraint the timetable might lay on the movements of his train. And the Great Western authorities, with publicity in mind, took great care to see that Rowe *should* be given the road. The upshot was that two of the journeys made by *Caldicot Castle* in this test week were two of the most astonishing feats for which "Castles" have ever been responsible.

On May 2nd Rowe took the "Limited" down to Plymouth, with the same loading as the Pacific, in 231 min. 58 sec., passing Westbury in 94 min. 40 sec. and Exeter in 169 min. 10 sec.; on April 27th, with one coach more than the Pacific, 358 tons tare and 380 tons gross, he came up from Exeter in 164 min. 1 sec. start to stop for the 173·7 miles. In both directions, therefore, Rowe had gained precisely 15 minutes on schedule. Moreover, despite the cost in coal consumption of such brilliant running, the 4-6-0 burned no more than 44·1, 45·6 and 46·8 lb. of coal to the mile going down, and 40·6, 36·8 and 37·9 lb. per mile coming up, the highest figure in each case being on the day when the gain of 15 minutes was being made. In both time and coal consumption, therefore, the "Castle" had beaten her rival handsomely on Great Western metals.

In qualification of these results, it may be added that the Pacific had to be restrained in her downhill speeds over the winding stretches of line from Reading onwards, due to her longer wheelbase (a matter which equally had troubled *The Great Bear* years before), and that Rowe took some of his speed restrictions, Reading in particular, at a speed considerably over the prescribed limits. Moreover, some of the Pacific's uphill work, notably a minimum speed of 32 m.p.h. over Dainton summit coming east with 310 tons, and, with the full 345 tons, the fine times of 22 minutes exactly from Exeter up the hill to Whiteball summit, and of no more than 26 min. 5 sec. for the 25·5 miles from Westbury up to Savernake (both exceptionally fast), was outstanding, even by Great Western standards. But even with allowance for these points, the "Castle" performance was well ahead of that of the Pacific.

To everyone's astonishment, the same took place on London & North Eastern metals, with Yorkshire coal. Certainly the L.N.E.R. made an unhappy choice of both engine and driver to compete with the "Castle" out of King's Cross, and though the running times were much closer, *Pendennis Castle* of the G.W.R. still had the best of it, not only in time but in coal consumption also. Though the blast and draught arrangements of a "Castle" are designed for Welsh coking coal, and the strong blast inevitably must increase coal consumption with a hard coal, Fireman Pearce mastered the art of firing with this unaccustomed fuel to such a degree as to keep his consumption with the 480-ton test loads to an average of 57·0 lb. per mile between King's Cross and Grantham, and 49·8 lb. per mile between King's Cross and Doncaster. Against this, Pacific No. 4475 *Flying Fox* was burning an average of 59·0 lb. per mile between London and Grantham and 55·3 lb. per mile between London and Doncaster. This gave the "Castles" an average advantage of 6 lb. per mile with Welsh coal and 3·7 lb. per mile with the Yorkshire product.

Moreover, Driver Young, with *Pendennis Castle*, again was winning in time with such feats as passing New Barnet, 67·2 miles from Peterborough, in 67 min. 45 sec. with a 485-ton train and reaching King's Cross in 77¾ minutes net; or in running from King's Cross to Peterborough, 76·4 miles, with 480 tons in 78 min. 50 sec. start to stop. The perfectly clean starts of the "Castle," especially up through the two greasy-railed tunnels out of King's Cross, were viewed with amazement by the L.N.E.R. authorities; who would have dreamed that this moderately-dimensioned 4-6-0 could lift 480-ton trains from King's Cross out through Finsbury Park in times of between 5¾ and 6 minutes, day after day, without the least suspicion of a slip? So the contest ended; the Great Western Railway had substantiated up to the very hilt their claim at the Wembley Exhibition, and did not fail to make all the capital they could in the *Great Western Railway Magazine* of the fact that their engine had "won," presenting the case in such terms as to end in friction what should have been a friendly exchange of knowledge.

[F. R. Hebron

"A1s" AT WORK—No. 2559 *The Tetrarch* attacks the long climb from Three Counties with an up Scotch express of 1926.

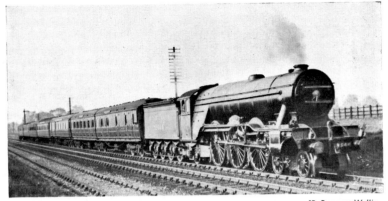

[*P. Ransome-Wallis*

FROM "A1" . . . No. 2544 *Lemberg*, with 18¼ in. diameter cylinders, working the "Scarborough Flyer" near Ranskill in 1928.

[*P. Ransome-Wallis*

"A1" No. 2562 *Isinglass* fitted with two snifting valves, during 1928 experiments with a 62-element superheater.

[*British Railways*

. . .TO "A3" The first of the new 220 lb. pressure "A3" Pacifics, No. 2743 *Felstead*, which appeared in 1928.

Coupled to a corridor tender, "A1" No. 4472 *Flying Scotsman* pulls out of King's Cross on May 1, 1928 with the first non-stop run of the 10 a.m. down to Edinburgh.

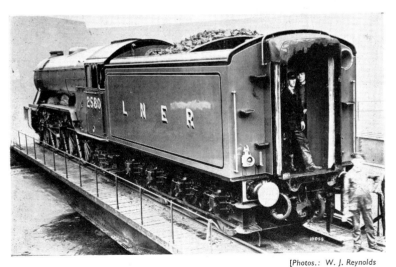

[Photos.: W. J. Reynolds

CORRIDOR TENDERS

Rear view of a corridor tender coupled to "A3" No. 2580 *Shotover*.

[F. R. Hebron

WITH WESTINGHOUSE BRAKE PUMP—No. 2575 *St. Frusquin*, one of the series of "A1s" built for the North Eastern Area, takes water from Langley troughs with the up "Flying Scotsman."

[P. Ransome-Wallis

WITH A.C.F.I. FEED WATER HEATER AND FEED-PUMP—"A3" No. 2580 *Shotover* was one of two Pacifics fitted with this apparatus in 1929.

4

The "A3" Pacifics

It might well be thought impossible for such an interchange trial as that of 1925 to take place without its results having some influence on subsequent L.N.E.R. locomotive practice. But this could not be regarded as a foregone conclusion. The only previous exchange in which a Great Western engine had participated, when the 4-cylinder 4-6-0 *Polar Star* ran over London & North Western metals in 1910, and in which the Swindon engine had proved devastatingly superior in capacity and efficiency to any L.N.W.R. express locomotive at that time, had had no influence whatever on L.N.W.R. locomotive design, so far as concerns front-end design or valve-setting. Even Gresley, big man though he was, still seemed disinclined to move, after the results of the 1925 exchange had been made public, until his chief technical assistant, Mr. B. Spencer, succeeded in persuading him to experiment with an improved valve-setting.

The remarkable fact is that a year before all this happened Gresley had given serious consideration to fitting the "A1" Pacifics with a long-lap valve-motion in order to permit of early cut-off working, evidently realising that while the engines were reliable enough, and more than competent to handle any task given them, their coal consumption was excessive. When designs were prepared for a modified gear, however, the scheme was dropped because of the expense involved in altering all the engines concerned; no more was done at that time than to give an additional lap of $\frac{1}{16}$ in. to the centre valve to counteract the over-running effect at high speed. Had the valve-gear change been made in 1924, the whole story of the famous exchange of 1925 might have been different; after the exchange was over, little excuse could remain for failing to make it.

As a first step, "A1" Pacific No. 4477 *Gay Crusader* was provided with valves having $1\frac{1}{2}$ in. in place of $1\frac{1}{4}$ in. lap, and though a minimum of alteration to the valve-gear had been made, the results were so satisfactory that the full modification envisaged in the 1924 design was now at last decided on. Pacific No. 2555 *Centenary* was the first to be given the redesigned valve-motion, with $1\frac{5}{8}$ in. lap, $\frac{1}{8}$ in. lead, and an increase in maximum valve travel from $4\frac{9}{16}$ in. to $5\frac{3}{4}$ in., still with a limitation of maximum cut-off to 65 per cent.; the additional $\frac{1}{16}$ in. of lap for the valve of the middle cylinder also was retained. The results were astonishing. As compared with the average coal consumption of the remaining "A1" Pacifics, *Centenary*, with the short cut-off working now made possible, brought the figure down from 50 to 38 lb. per mile, which meant an economy of 33 cwt. on a single round trip from Doncaster to King's Cross and back. Eventually, all the other "A1" Pacifics were modified in the same way as they came into "Plant" for heavy repairs, and the redesigned gear became the standard for future Pacific construction.

But the other lesson of the 1925 exchange—that of high working pressures, one of the secrets of the Great Western success—had yet to be applied, and in this matter Gresley did not move until 1927. In that year two of the "A1" Pacifics emerged from Doncaster Works with new boilers in which the pressure was increased from 180 to 220 lb. per sq. in. With this alteration came the provision of a larger superheater, 43 elements instead of 32, which increased the superheating surface from 525 to 706 sq. ft., while the tube heating surface was reduced from 2,715 to 2,477 sq. ft. Other boiler dimensions remained unaltered, except for an increase in the thickness of the boiler-plates and a closer pitching of the firebox stays, to withstand the higher pressure. The two engines concerned were No. 2544 *Lemberg* and No. 4480 *Enterprise*.

While *Enterprise* retained her 20 in. diameter cylinders, *Lemberg* had hers lined up to $18\frac{1}{4}$ inches: the former thus had her tractive effort increased to 36,465 lb., while in the latter the reduction in cylinder diameter roughly balanced the increased boiler pressure, and left the tractive effort at much the same level as before, actually now 30,360 lb. Between the work of the two engines there was little difference; only on starting, or at other times when exceptional effort was required, did the larger cylinders of *Enterprise* give her the advantage.

On the other hand, in those days I always found *Lemberg* to be an exceptionally fast engine when sustained high speed was needed. The alterations to *Enterprise* put the weight of the engine up from 92½ to 96¼ tons, and to maintain the previous ratio of tractive effort to adhesion, the weight distribution was modified to increase the adhesion weight from 60 to 66¼ tons. Later in 1927 Nos. 2573 *Harvester*, 2578 *Bayardo* and 2580 *Shotover* were rebuilt similarly to *Enterprise*.

Soon after the conversion of *Enterprise* I had the opportunity of making some trips with her on the footplate, and the change on driving method from the handling of "A1" Pacific *Solario*, as described in Chapter 2, was striking indeed. Going north on the 5.45 p.m. from King's Cross, with a 460-ton train, we had come down to 30 per cent. cut-off by the top of the 1 in 105 at Holloway, and this was enough to get us through Finsbury Park in 5½ minutes exactly. By Hornsey we were down to 15 per cent., and the driver then gradually advanced to 20 per cent. up the long 1 in 200 to Potter's Bar; for most of the distance from here on to Peterborough, 13 to 15 per cent., instead of *Solario's* 45 per cent., was the working position, with the regulator partly closed on the downhill lengths, and the Peterborough stop was reached easily in 83 min. 50 sec.

Much the same thing happened on the 10.10 a.m. from King's Cross, with a 440-ton train; again we cleared Finsbury Park in 5½ minutes, this time with 40 per cent. cut-off at the top of Holloway bank; 22 per cent. was used up to Potter's Bar and 15 per cent. for most of the remainder of the run. In the up direction, similar methods of working brought a 315-ton train through New Barnet, 96·3 miles from Grantham, in 99 min. 10 sec., with no maximum speed higher than 72½ m.p.h., and we reached London in 109 min. 30 sec., or 108¾ minutes net for the 105·5 miles. On this run the steam-chest pressure gauge showed that, whenever the engine was working hard, the pressure in the steam-chest was within about 90 per cent. of the actual boiler pressure—a testimony to the care that had been bestowed on the design and layout of the steam passages.

In February, 1928, comparative tests were carried out with the dynamometer car between King's Cross and Doncaster in which *Lemberg* was pitted against No. 4473 *Solario*, the former with 220 lb. pressure and 18¼ in. cylinders and the latter with

180 lb. pressure and 20 in. cylinders. Each was tested for a full week, with average tare loads of 428 and 435 tons respectively on the up journey, 506 and 491 tons from King's Cross to Peterborough, and 348 and 331 tons from Peterborough to Doncaster. Average coal consumptions were 35·37 and 38·83 lb. per mile in favour of the high pressure Pacific, and water consumption 288·8 against 317·5 lb. per mile, while *Lemberg* also was making the higher average speeds, 56·84 against 54·93 m.p.h. coming up and 52·54 against 50·73 m.p.h. going down. But *Solario* had to battle with bad weather conditions, with the result that the average coal consumptions per drawbar horse-power-hour were almost identical, 3·11 lb. with *Lemberg* and 3·07 lb. with *Solario*— a curiously inconclusive outcome. It is difficult to understand why *Enterprise*, with the larger cylinders, was not included in these comparative trials.

In any event, the working of the 220 lb. Pacifics was regarded as sufficiently satisfactory to justify the introduction of the higher working pressure and enlarged superheater; if the change did nothing else, it gave the Pacifics an increased starting tractive effort to compensate in a measure for what they had lost by the limitation of maximum cut-off to 65 per cent. So the building of the first "A3" Pacifics was decided on, and now it could be claimed that the lessons of the 1925 exchange had been applied in full. But in one respect the new Gresley practice was diametrically opposed to that of the G.W.R. In 1927 Collett, who had completed at Swindon his first 4-6-0 "King," with working pressure raised still further to 250 lb., had retained the same 16-element superheater—or, more precisely, steam-dryer—that had been used in his previous "Castles," carrying no more than 225 lb. pressure. Gresley, on the other hand, in increasing his working pressure from 180 to 220 lb. per sq. in., had increased his superheater at the same time from 32 to 43 elements, and, so far as concerned the Yorkshire coal normally used, the working of the "A3" Pacifics has fully justified his high temperature superheat.

It may be added that in 1926 Gresley experimented on No. 2562 *Isinglass* with an even larger "E" type superheater having no fewer than 62 elements, but as compared with "A1" Pacific No. 2570 *Tranquil*, which had a 32-element superheater, the gain in average superheat temperature was no more than 31 deg. F. The 43-element superheater finally standardised in 1928 for the "A3" Pacifics therefore was regarded as adequate. Its presence became apparent externally by the large patch on each side of the smokebox, housing the outer ends of the superheater header.

The first new Pacifics to be built with 220 lb. boilers, to the "A3" design, were headed by No. 2743 *Felstead*, which emerged from Doncaster Works in August, 1928; they were numbered from 2743 to 2752 inclusive. Six were completed in 1928, and the remaining four in 1929. Gresley had decided to split the difference between the 20 in. cylinders of *Enterprise* and the $18\frac{1}{4}$ in. cylinders of *Lemberg*, and to standardise on 19 in. with the new "A3" series. This gave a tractive effort, at 85 per cent. of the boiler pressure, of 32,910 lb. The $5\frac{3}{4}$ in. valve-travel and $1\frac{5}{8}$ in. lap remained standard, as also the 8 in. piston-valves. In common with a change which was now taking place all over the country, the driving position was altered from the right-hand to the left-hand side of the cab.

Another development about this time was the equipment of some of the Pacifics with corridor tenders. One phase of the inter-group competition already referred to had been as to which group could run the longest distance without stop. In 1927 the L.N.E.R. had begun by working the 9.50 a.m. relief "Scotsman" non-stop over the 268·3 miles between King's Cross and Newcastle, while the L.M.S.R. was running the 236·3 miles from Euston to Carnforth with the "Royal Scot"; on receipt of its new "Royal Scot" 4-6-0 engines the L.M.S.R. had extended its run from Euston through to Carlisle, 299·1 miles; and the L.N.E.R., from May 1st, 1928, had countered by booking the "Flying Scotsman" non-stop over the 392·7 miles between King's Cross and Edinburgh—a feat, incidentally, which would have been difficult, if not impossible, of accomplishment but for the economical engine working made possible by the valve gear modifications that followed the 1925 locomotive exchange. For this latter run it became necessary to provide means whereby the engine-crew could be changed at the midway point on the run, just north of York, without stopping the train; and this was the genesis of Gresley's unique corridor tenders.

THE GRESLEY PACIFICS OF THE L.N.E.R.

The first five Pacifics to be provided with them were No. 4472 *Flying Scotsman*, No. 4476 *Royal Lancer*, No. 2573 *Harvester*, No. 2577 *Night Hawk*, and No. 2580 *Shotover*. Each of these tenders is 25 ft. 10 in. long, and is provided with a passage 18 in. wide and 5 ft. high running along the right-hand side. At the rear end of the tender there is a Pullman vestibule connection exactly similar to that of a coach; starting from this the corridor turns sharp right, and then sharp left at the corner of the tender, which is fitted with a circular window to provide light. When fully charged with 9 tons of coal and 5,000 gallons of water, each of these massive tenders weighs 62½ tons, increasing the weight of an "A3" Pacific with tender to 158¾ tons. More corridor tenders were built after the introduction of the "A4" Pacifics, and the total number, all now attached to engines of the "A4" type, is twenty.

In the year 1929, when the A.C.F.I. feed-water heating apparatus was under trial on *ex*-Great Eastern 4-6-0 engines of the "B12" class and on *ex*-North Eastern Atlantics of the "C7" class, Gresley decided on a similar experiment with Pacifics, two of which were fitted, "A1" class No. 2576 *The White Knight* and "A3" class No. 2580 *Shotover*. As with boilers of this size there was no room for the heaters in the usual position on both sides of the boiler barrel between chimney and dome, a special type of heater was designed to occupy the upper part of the smokebox and projecting as a kind of half-moon above it almost up to the height of the chimney, giving the engines concerned a curiously massive appearance at the front end. Tests proved that the apparatus could deliver feed into the boiler (by means of a feed-pump, of course) at temperatures up to 225 deg. F. The two engines carried the apparatus for some years, but nothing came of the experiment.

The value of the 220 lb. boiler of the "A3" Pacifics in promoting more efficient working now became so well established as to promote the decision to rebuild all the 52 "A1" Pacifics into Class "A3" as reboilering became necessary. The matter of conversion was held up for a time during the Second World War; and after the war, with the emergence of new Pacific types under Gresley's successors, the remaining engines of Class "A1" by then had been re-classified as

"A10." The last conversion from Class "A10" to Class "A3," that of *Sir Visto* (originally No. 2567, later No. 68, and finally No. 60068) did not take place until 1949. None of the Gresley Pacifics now remains in the original "A1" form, with 180 lb. pressure. *Enterprise* and *Lemberg* also have long since received the standard 19 in. cylinders of the "A3" class.

In 1930 eight more "A3" Pacifics made their appearance; all were built at Doncaster, and the numbers were 2595 to 2599 inclusive, and 2795, 2796 and 2797. With these engines there was introduced a new type of tender, with curved tops to the side-sheets, like those of the corridor tenders, and high curved rear ends. This was one only of various tender modifications of later years, such as the streamlined tenders built for the "A4" Pacifics, to which pattern all the corridor tenders were altered eventually, and the streamlined version of the non-corridor tenders that appeared at a still later date. The last of the "A3s" were built in 1934 (except No. 2508 *Brown Jack*, which appeared in 1935), nine in all numbered from 2500 to 2508 inclusive, bringing the total of "A3" engines built as such to 27, and of all the Gresley Pacifics to 79.

The final batch, beginning with No. 2500 *Windsor Lad*, had their domes replaced by a new type of steam collector, shaped like a banjo, into which steam passes through longitudinal slots in the top of the boiler barrel rather than through the usual circular opening, with a view to the prevention of priming. This "banjo dome," which has since become a standard fitting, was shifted back from the usual dome position astride the joint between the second and third rings of the boiler barrel to the middle of the third ring, with quite a perceptible effect on the appearance of the engines. In fact, this change began a deterioration in the fine external lines of the original "A1" series which has continued apace with each successive modification.

Some of the performances put up by the "A1" and "A3" Pacifics figure in a later chapter; but before that we have to deal with the circumstances which helped to produce the most famous of all the Gresley designs, the streamlined "A4," that has been responsible for not a few of the most outstanding feats of performance in British locomotive history.

5

Preparing for the Streamliners

The period between 1930 and 1939 marked a sudden and startling advance in railway speed all over the world. In Great Britain it began, in 1932, with the abandonment by the L.M.S.R. and L.N.E.R. of the long-standing agreement which had tied down the minimum times between London and both Glasgow and Edinburgh to the 8 hours, 15 minutes laid down after the Race to Aberdeen in 1895. How absurd such a limitation had become had been abundantly clear when in the summer of 1928 all intermediate stops had been taken out of the run of the "Flying Scotsman" between King's Cross and Edinburgh, but the engines had still been compelled to dawdle along at a much reduced speed in order to fill out the unchanged $8\frac{1}{4}$ hours allowance. In the very first year of the acceleration, the non-stop timing was cut by no less than 45 minutes at one stroke, bringing it down to $7\frac{1}{2}$ hours, and this was reduced successively to $7\frac{1}{4}$ hours in 1936 and 7 hours in 1937. At the same time the speeds of other expresses were being increased considerably, and runs timed at a mile-a-minute and more from start to stop were beginning to appear in the timetables.

Meantime the development overseas of other forms of motive power for the working of high speed passenger services was coming prominently under notice. By 1932 the German State Railways had introduced their "Fliegende Hamburger" two-car streamline train, and by 1933 they were running it every day from Berlin to Hamburg at an average speed of 77·4 m.p.h.—178·1 miles in 138 minutes—a schedule which, with allowance for speed restrictions, required regular running speeds up to 100 m.p.h. In the United States in 1934 similar and more capacious diesel streamliners, the "Pioneer Zephyr" of the Chicago, Burlington & Quincy Railroad and the "City of Portland" of the Union Pacific, had taken the whole of that country by storm, and had set on foot a change in motive power on American railways on a scale which, fifteen years later, seems almost unbelievable in so short a time. It is not surprising, therefore, that, with a British public now speed-conscious, questions began to be asked as to why we could not see some similar enterprise in this country.

The answer was that Great Britain, with abundant supplies of the best steam coal in the world, would be foolish to abandon this fuel in favour of imported oil for the running of its trains. But Gresley did not leave the matter there. In 1934 he obtained estimates from the German builders of the "Flying Hamburger" unit as to the time which, in their estimation, would be needed to travel between London and Newcastle by a three-car train with similar diesel-electric power, taking all speed restrictions into account. After a study of the physical characteristics of the route, the time stated by the German firm, for a train of 115 tons weight, seating 140 passengers, was $4\frac{1}{4}$ hours. Gresley, convinced that a similar time could be maintained reliably by steam power, decided to make some preliminary experiments with Pacifics in order to prove his point; for one of these, between King's Cross and Leeds, an "A1" Pacific was turned out, and for the other, over the full King's Cross—Newcastle course, an "A3."

So it was that on a dull and misty November morning in 1934—actually November 30th—I found myself in the "Local" Station at King's Cross, in company with a few officials, stepping into a four-coach train which had been marshalled for the run to Leeds. At the head of it was No. 4472 *Flying Scotsman*, and on the footplate the famous Bill Sparshatt with his Fireman Webster, about to give us a run of a speed quality undreamed of even over L.N.E.R. metals up to that time. In retrospect, it is, perhaps, remarkable that we got any further than the mouth of Gasworks Tunnel that morning. For the engine, with so short a train, was well back along the platform, and Sparshatt opened up with such vigour that when we reached the sharp and awkward connections leading from the platform out on to the main line, the engine was travelling at such a speed as to leave flange-marks on rails in positions where flanges certainly are not expected to run. Mercifully, however, nothing worse happened, and so we were away.

With a load of no more than 147 tons, *Flying Scotsman* now

treated us to a display of unprecedented brilliance. Little notice was taken of the tentative schedule prepared; the engine was given her head, and the operating authorities played the game magnificently by keeping the road ahead of us perfectly clear. What a thrill it was! We were through Finsbury Park in just over 4 minutes and Hatfield in just over 17 minutes; $71\frac{1}{2}$ m.p.h. was the speed through Wood Green and 67-$68\frac{1}{2}$ m.p.h. all the way up the 1 in 200 to Potter's Bar; next followed 83 through Hatfield and $93\frac{1}{2}$ through Hitchin; and then 86 to 95 all the way until we eased for the Offord curves. So we were through Hitchin in 28 min. 22 sec., Huntingdon in 46 min. 31 sec., and Peterborough in no more than 39 seconds over the even hour—for the first 76·4 miles! On the down journey Sparshatt had not allowed his engine to exceed the 95 m.p.h. reached just after Hitchin.

After recovery from the Peterborough slack, which was rigidly observed, right down to 21 m.p.h., there came an ascent to Stoke Summit which, mile by mile as we made it, seemed completely unbelievable. We were to get used to these things later on, as the streamliners came into regular service, but on this first 80 m.p.h. flight on record "up the hill," it might well have been thought that the grade had flattened out to zero, for all the notice Sparshatt and his engine took of it. By Werrington Junction we were doing $71\frac{1}{2}$ m.p.h. and by Tallington 79; up the 1 in 440 and 264 to Essendine speed increased to 84; the minimum up the $4\frac{1}{2}$ miles at 1 in 200 to milepost $95\frac{1}{2}$ was a steady $82\frac{1}{4}$; and after a momentary increase to 83 on the easier $1\frac{1}{2}$ miles to Corby Glen, we stormed the last 3 miles of 1 in 178 to the summit, now with *Flying Scotsman* cutting off at 40 per cent., at an absolute minimum of 81 m.p.h. The ten miles' climb between the 90th and 100th mileposts had been made at an *average* speed of $82\frac{1}{2}$ miles an hour !

So the special was whirled over the 29·1 miles from Peterborough to Grantham in 23 minutes to the dead second. The schedule had allowed us 26 minutes, and on passing Grantham, 105·5 miles, in 83 min. 39 sec. from King's Cross, we were nearly $8\frac{1}{2}$ minutes ahead of time. Still the road remained clear. From here the running was perhaps a shade easier; otherwise I verily believe we should have been through

Doncaster in a "record-of-records" time of two hours from London; as it was, we were passing the 153¾ milepost at the precise end of the second hour. Two independent stages of the journey had been completed at average speeds of over 80 m.p.h.—the 70·0 miles from Wood Green to Fletton Junction at 80·8, and now the 71·3 miles from Helpston to Black Carr Junction—Stoke Summit included—at 80·3 m.p.h. Doncaster, 156·0 miles, was passed in 122 min. 27 sec. from King's Cross.

Relatively to the steepness of the gradients, Sparshatt treated us to some more amazing speed after Doncaster; 2¾ miles at 1 in 150 up past South Elmsall dropped the speed no more than from 80 to 77½ m.p.h., and the final 1¼ miles at the same inclination to Nostell Summit from 81 to 77½ m.p.h., while to finish the 1 in 100-122 to Ardsley Summit at 55½ m.p.h. was another extraordinary experience. Up several uphill lengths on which minimum speeds were a full 50 per cent. and more higher than those normally run, we experienced lurches on curves of which we had barely suspected the existence previously. Who would have conceived possible a time of no more than 17 min. 1 sec. for the 19·9 miles from Doncaster to Wakefield, begun at 40 m.p.h. and ended at 35? Finally, after the usual 10 m.p.h. slack through Holbeck, *Flying Scotsman* drew up in Leeds Central 2 hours, 31 minutes, 56 seconds after leaving King's Cross. As previously indicated, Sparshatt would have had little difficulty in cutting this to the even 2½ hours; as it was, we had pared our 2¾-hour schedule by a full 13 minutes.

The seating accommodation on the down journey (had a third-class brake replaced the dynamometer car) would roughly have equalled the 102 seats in the twin-unit German "Fliegende Hamburger," but our train had a proper restaurant car as compared with the German train's cold buffet only. From Leeds to London, however, in order to simulate a train of the accommodation that might be needed for a high-speed London—Leeds or London—Newcastle service, two corridor thirds were added, bringing the seating up to more than double that of the "Fliegende Hamburger." We were booked out of Leeds at 2 p.m., and this fact brought back vivid memories of Great Northern days, when Ivatt Atlantics used to leave Leeds

TABLE I.

Test Runs between London and Leeds, November 30th, 1934

Engine: "A1" 4-6-2 No. 4472, *Flying Scotsman*

145 tons tare, 147 tons full					205 tons tare, 207 tons full			
Dist.	Sched.	Actual	Speeds		Dist.	Sched.	Actual	Speeds
miles	min.	min. sec.	m.p.h.		miles	min.	min. sec.	m.p.h.
0·0	0	0 00	—	KING'S CROSS	185·8	165	157 17	—
2·5	—	4 04	55	FINSBURY PARK	183·3	—	153 22	—
5·0	—	6 25	71½	Wood Green	180·8	—	151 13	81
9·2	—	10 07	68½	New Barnet	176·6	—	148 08	80
12·7	—	13 16	67	Potter's Bar	173·1	—	145 16	70
17·7	19	17 03	83	HATFIELD	168·1	148	141 11	85
23·5	—	22 06	†60/68½	*Woolmer Green*	162·3	—	136 48	72
28·6	—	26 05	80	Stevenage	157·2	—	132 37	70/76
31·9	30	28 22	93½	HITCHIN	153·9	137	129 50	72½
37·0	—	31 40	95/86	Arlesey	148·8	—	125 38	75/76½
41·1	—	34 27	92	Biggleswade	144·7	—	122 00	62
44·1	—	36 24	92½	Sandy	141·7	—	118 33	*40
47·5	—	38 38	93	Tempsford	138·3	—	115 55	81
51·7	—	41 29	85	St. Neot's	134·1	—	112 38	71½
56·0	—	44 24	90/*78	Offord	129·8	—	109 08	eased
58·9	50	46 31	82	HUNTINGDON	126·9	116	106 42	80½
62·0	—	48 58	72½	*Milepost 62*	123·8	—	104 13	72
69·4	—	54 28	83	Holme	116·4	—	98 31	83
75·0	—	58 57	—	*Fletton Junction*	110·8	—	93 52	—
76·4	66	60 39	*21	PETERBOROUHH	109·4	100	92 00	*25
79·5	—	64 20	71½	*Werrington Junction*	106·3	—	89 00	80
84·8	—	68 26	80	Tallington	101·0	—	85 10	86½
88·6	—	71 13	84	Essendine	97·2	—	82 38	100
92·2	—	73 47	84	Little Bytham	93·6	—	80 25	95½
97·1	—	77 21	82	Corby Glen	88·7	—	77 11	86
100·1	—	79 33	81	*Stoke*	85·7	—	74 54	68½
105·5	92	83 39	87/*62	GRANTHAM	80·3	74	70 18	73¾
109·7	—	87 16	—	Barkstone	76·1	—	66 45	69
115·4	—	91 24	90	Claypole	70·4	—	62 13	78
120·1	103	94 38	86½	NEWARK	65·7	62	58 28	77½
126·4	—	99 10	82½	Carlton	59·4	—	53 01	82
133·7	—	104 53	76½	*Markham*	52·1	—	48 23	74
138·6	119	108 44	84/*69	RETFORD	47·2	47	44 28	81½
143·9	—	112 53	87	Ranskill	41·9	—	40 41	86½
149·5	—	116 50	88/79	*Milepost 149½*	36·3	—	36 44	73/88
153·2	—	119 31	87	*Black Carr Junction*	32·6	—	33 49	77½
156·0	133	122 27	*40	DONCASTER	29·8	32	30 58	*35
160·0	—	126 38	76	Carcroft	25·8	—	27 01	*72
164·7	—	130 17	80/77½	South Elmsall	21·1	—	23 25	77½/82
167·9	—	132 41	81	Hemsworth	17·9	—	20 47	74½
170·4	—	134 37	77½	Nostell	15·4	—	18 33	61½
174·2	—	137 26	83	Sandal	11·6	—	14 55	64
175·9	151	139 28	*35	WAKEFIELD	9·9	14	12 42	*39
178·3	—	141 22	57/*40	Lofthouse	7·5	—	9 46	*48
180·2	157	144 39	55½	Ardsley	5·6	9	7 46	54
183·3	—	147 46	68	Beeston	2·5	—	4 17	56
185·3	—	150 15	*10	Holbeck	0·5	—	1 36	—
185·8	165	151 56	—	LEEDS CENTRAL	0·0	0	0 00	—

*Speed restriction. † Speed reduction by brakes leaking on slightly.

Central at precisely the same hour with the famous "Special Express" that was due in King's Cross at 5.27 p.m. That was with five coaches; to-day we were destined to bring six coaches into the London terminus fifty minutes earlier!

In Table 1 I have given the principal details of the up run, as of the down. The engine seemed just as much at home with the heavier train, and there were some even more brilliant exploits, as, for example, the way in which we recovered from 35 m.p.h. through Doncaster to $77\frac{1}{2}$ by Rossington, took Piper's Wood "hump" at 73, and were up to 88 by Scrooby troughs—all in ten miles! Minima of 74 m.p.h. over Markham Summit (following $81\frac{1}{2}$ over Retford level crossing!), 69 at Peascliffe Tunnel, and $68\frac{1}{2}$ at Stoke Summit were all excellent with a 208-ton load. To Grantham we ran the 80·3 miles from Leeds, including the steep climb from the start and the Wakefield and Doncaster slacks, in 70 min. 18 sec.; the test schedule was 74 minutes.

Now *Flying Scotsman* went like the wind. Down from Stoke Summit the fastest quarter-miles that I "clocked" were two at $97\frac{1}{2}$ m.p.h., and this was the figure quoted in a hurriedly-prepared broadcast of the day's events that I gave that evening as part of the "nine o'clock news." But closer examination of the dynamometer car roll showed that for a very short distance, between Little Bytham and Essendine, the magic "100" line had been reached—a climax indeed to the engine's exploits. On passing Peterborough, in 92 minutes to the second from Leeds, we were 8 minutes ahead of time.

By now Fireman Webster was tiring, and small wonder! In the whole of this strenuous day he shovelled all but 9 tons of coal into the firebox of the engine, with no more rest between the two $2\frac{1}{2}$-hour continuous spells of firing than the two hours we had spent in Leeds. So, between Peterborough and London, Sparshatt held pretty closely to his point-to-point bookings, and eventually we came to a stand in King's Cross at just after 4.37 p.m., in 2 hours, 37 minutes, 17 seconds from Leeds. Our amazing engine and her crew had spent exactly 250 miles out of a single day's duty travelling at a mean speed of 80 miles an hour! Their return journey of 371·6 miles had occupied 9 minutes, 13 seconds over five hours! This made it clear that steam was capable of equalling any diesel-electric performance up to that date.

More concrete proposals soon began to emerge. History does not relate from whom the initiative came, but there is every reason to believe that Gresley was responsible; and fortunately he had a Chief General Manager and a Board of Directors who were anything but hidebound by conservatism, and were quite prepared to make any move which would enhance the prestige of the London & North Eastern Railway. Early in 1935, therefore, the decision was reached to build a steam-hauled streamline train, the first in Britain, which daily would bridge the 268·3 miles between London and Newcastle in four hours each way.

A second test trip therefore was planned for March 5th, 1935, on which the King's Cross—Newcastle journey would be made in each direction non-stop in four hours. Whereas the London—Leeds test of the previous November had been made with an "A1" Pacific, and 180 lb. pressure, on this second run it was decided that the engine used should be a 220 lb. "A3." No. 2750 *Papyrus* was the locomotive selected, and she was destined to have an extremely strenuous day. In the down direction, Driver Gutteridge and Fireman Wightman of King's Cross shed would officiate; coming back, they would turn over the engine to the record-breaking Sparshatt-Webster combination. The load was six coaches, of 213 tons tare and 217 tons gross.

With recollections of the previous November's all but disastrous exit from No. 11 platform at King's Cross, the authorities wisely switched the March special into No. 10, so that we had a reasonably straight start. Going down, Gutteridge did not allow the speed to exceed 88½ m.p.h. at any point; 80½ at Hatfield, 88½ at Three Counties, 86 at Tempsford, 81 at Tallington, 83¼ at Claypole, and 80 at both Gamston and Black Carr Junction, were the highest speeds south of Doncaster. Allowing for the heavier load, the uphill work probably equalled that of *Flying Scotsman* in the previous test, for from Essendine to Stoke speed remained steadily at between 75 and 77½ m.p.h. The running was an almost exact forecast of what would become a daily perform-ance in the streamline era; Peterborough was passed in

63 min. 21 sec., Grantham in 87 min. 42 sec., Retford in 115 min. 18 sec., and Black Carr Junction, 153·2 miles, in 127 min. 39 sec.

Now came an unexpected incident. The approach to Doncaster was heralded by prolonged whistling, for signals were against us. Slowing down almost to walking pace, Gutteridge picked up a pilotman, who informed him that that morning a freight train had distributed itself over the track near Arksey, and that single line working was in force. At Moat Hills box (156·8 miles) we came to a dead stand, but fortunately for no more than 19 seconds. From Arksey, passed at a walking pace, *Papyrus* did a fine bit of acceleration, getting up to 85 m.p.h. in no more than 8 miles of dead level track. As a result, we were through York in 165 min. 11 sec., just over a minute late. Two years later, the "Coronation" was due to begin running to York every day in 157 minutes, with a load of no less than 325 tons against our 217 tons. Such is the march of time—and railway speed!

From York we bowled along happily over the Great Plain of York at between 79 and 85 m.p.h. all the way from Beningbrough to Northallerton, and after severe slowings past Browney Colliery, Durham and Lamesley, drew into the Central Station at Newcastle in 237 minutes 7 seconds from London, 3 minutes early; our net time had been 230 minutes for the 268·3 miles from London. *Papyrus* and her passengers now had a rest of 2¾ hours before we started back; no decision had been reached in advance as to what engine would be used for the up journey, but our "A3" was perfectly cool and in excellent running order, so it was decided that *Papyrus* should be used up as well as down. Prompt to time at 3.47 p.m. we started, with Sparshatt now in charge.

For Sparshatt, the going was distinctly leisurely as far as Ferryhill, to which point we lost 1¾ minutes, but then we were treated to some grand running; the next 55·4 miles, to Poppleton Junction, were reeled off in 41 min. 28 sec., with a sustained 80 to 88 m.p.h. for the 33 miles from Danby Wiske onwards. This took us through York in 72 min. 17 sec. from Newcastle (80·1 miles); continuing, we passed Shaftholme

Junction, 108·1 miles, in 99 min. 3 sec., 4 minutes early. What of the derailed freighter? By now, fortunately, the up road was clear, though very cautious running was still needed past the site of the derailment; as a result, our gain had been all but wiped out as we passed Doncaster, once again on time.

From Doncaster to Grantham, Sparshatt was content to "nurse" his engine, in preparation for the record speed which it was certainly intended to attempt on the descent from Stoke. We ran well, keeping closely to booked point-to-point times, and so passing Grantham in 148 min. 42 sec. Now *Papyrus* was opened out. Up the long 1 in 200 to Stoke there was very little variation in speed, no more than from 71½ to 69 m.p.h. Down the far side we accelerated like a rocket; by Little Bytham we were well over the "100" line; and finally there came the "peak" of 108.

This was no mere sudden spurt; for more than 2 miles I was reading 105 m.p.h. or over, and we averaged 105·4 m.p.h. from Little Bytham to Essendine and 100·6 on to Tallington; indeed, for 12·3 miles, from Corby to Tallington, our mean speed was 100·6 m.p.h. So we brought the Grantham—Peterborough time down to the amazing figure of 21 minutes (*plus* one second!), gaining no less than 5 minutes on the test schedule between these two points alone. To the recorders the thrill of such a flight, far faster than anything they had clocked before, may be imagined.

The engine stood it all magnificently, and seemed game to carry on indefinitely; from Peterborough to London the time was the fastest on record up to that date. The 76·4 miles to King's Cross were run in 62 min. 6 sec., so that we stopped under the terminus roof in 231 min. 48 sec. from our Newcastle start. Of the tail end of the run the most remarkable feature was the time of 20 min. 17 sec. for the 27·0 miles from Huntingdon to Hitchin, largely uphill, with speed as high as 87 m.p.h. before Sandy; at the finish of the long 1 in 200 climb, on passing Stevenage, we were doing 78 m.p.h.

What a day it had been! Our "A3" Pacific had run 500 miles from King's Cross to Croxdale (just south of Durham) and back in 423 min. 57 sec., or (allowing for the two Arksey

[*P. Ransome-Wallis*

The 1934 "A3s" appeared with a banjo-shaped steam collector, placed farther to the rear of the boiler.   No. 2502 *Hyperion* was one of this batch.   Note also the high-sided non-corridor tender first seen on Nos. 2595-9 in 1930.

[*F. R. Hebron*

"BANJO DOME"

This is now a standard fitting, and can be seen on "A3" No. 56 *Centenary*, a rebuilt "A1," heading north through Welwyn with a Sunday King's Cross—Hull express.

EXPERIMENTS IN
SMOKE
DEFLECTION

(Left) "A3" No. 2747
Coronach, as running in
1932.

(Centre) "A3" No. 2751
Humorist in 1932.

(Bottom) No. 2751, as
running from 1937-47,
with double-chimney.

[Photos.: W. J. Reynolds
(left), P. Ransome-Wallis

[*P. Ransome-Wallis*

HUMORIST TO-DAY—Now renumbered 60097, *Humorist* keeps its double-chimney, but is fitted with standard E.R. smoke deflectors of the type seen on Thompson & Peppercorn Pacifics.

[*F. R. Hebron*

FILM STAR—No. 4472 heads the "Flying Scotsman" train past Palmers Green on a 1928 trip down the Hertford branch for film-making at Watton, Hertfordshire.

delays) 412½ minutes net, at an average of 72·7 m.p.h. for the entire distance. Some 121 miles of the down journey and 179 miles of the up, 300 miles all told, had been covered at a mean rate of 80 m.p.h. Yes, the two engine-crews and *Papyrus*, with the help of perfect control of the traffic over the whole length of the main line, had proved that a 4-hour schedule was perfectly feasible. The stage had been set for the "A4" Pacifics and for the streamline trains.

(Illustrations on facing page)

THE FINAL RE-BUILDING

(Top) No. 4470 *Great Northern*, as originally built, tops the rise at Potters Bar with the 5.45 p.m. King's Cross—Leeds and Bradford express in 1928.

[*F. R. Hebron*

(Centre) No. 4470 as first rebuilt by Thompson, without deflectors and with shallow cab.

[*British Railways*

(Bottom) No. 4470 as Class "A1/1," with modified cab and smoke deflectors.

[*P. Ransome-Wallis*

6

The "A4" Pacifics

If ever a convincing proof were needed of my earlier contention that when Gresley designed a locomotive, it went straight out on to the line to take up, with complete success and reliability, the service for which he had evolved the design, it may be found in the *début* of the first streamlined "A4" Pacific, No. 2509 *Silver Link*. Once again his drawing office staff had done their work thoroughly and well; all the necessary thinking and experimenting were over before the engine took the road; and this competence in design had been backed by first-class Doncaster workmanship.

For within three weeks of the emergence from Doncaster of this remarkable vision of silver and grey, the new engine had achieved by far the most dazzling feat of British railway speed up to that date, which may remain unequalled, let alone unbeaten, for many years to come. Moreover, as no second engine of the class was ready, *Silver Link* three days later began to work the new streamline train, the "Silver Jubilee," *in both directions daily*, five days a week, for the next fortnight without any relief—a duty which required the locomotive to make *two* 232-mile non-stop runs each day at a scheduled average speed of 70·4 m.p.h. from start to stop! To such a *première* as this British locomotive history finds no parallel whatever.

In the "A4" Pacifics, Gresley had reached the crowning achievement of his distinguished career. Later, while on the one hand *Mallard* was to achieve a world speed record for steam by attaining a maximum speed of 126 m.p.h., other "A4" Pacifics were to prove that the competence of the class was by no means confined to the haulage of lightweight streamline trains. Ultimately they were to be faced with such tasks as running the " Flying Scotsman," with a load of 550 tons and even more, over the 105·5 miles from Grantham to King's Cross in 105½ minutes every day. In the early stages of the Second World War *Silver Link* herself was to take from King's Cross to Newcastle, unassisted, a train of 25 bogie coaches, weighing, with its crowded passenger complement, fully 850 tons behind the tender.

And even to-day, years after Gresley's untimely death, and notwithstanding the efforts of his successors to improve the master's work, if any Eastern Region engine is needed for a major task, it is on a Gresley "A4" that the choice falls. This was seen on the experimental high speed run from King's Cross in May, 1946, when it was not the rebuilt No. 4470 *Great Northern* that was selected, but No. 2512 *Silver Fox*. Again, in the extensive locomotive exchange trials of 1948, when the Eastern Region had available both the rebuilt *Great Northern* and the new "A2" Pacific designs, Gresley "A4" Pacifics, unaltered from the original "A4" design in any respect other than Gresley's addition of the Kylchap exhaust and double chimney, were the engines chosen to uphold the reputation of the Eastern Region of British Railways.

We come now to the details of the "A4" design. While the general layout, including wheelbase, motion details, boiler diameters, and so on, was identical with that of the "A1" and "A3" Pacifics, there were notable differences. Of these the most striking, of course, was appearance. Notwithstanding the successful trial with *Papyrus* on the proposed 4-hour schedule between London and Newcastle, Gresley realised that, to maintain such speeds in all weathers, a margin of power would be needed, and that any assistance which it was possible to give the engine, by reducing both internal and external resistance, would be of value. Streamlining both locomotive and train immediately suggested themselves as an aid in this direction, in view of the high continuous speeds contemplated; and such an addition would be likely to have publicity value also.

In the typical atmospheric conditions of these islands, it would be vitally necessary so to design the streamlining that when the locomotive was working at high speed, on a short cut-off, the smoke and exhaust steam would be lifted clear of the cab windows. Exhaustive wind tunnel experiments were carried out at the City and Guilds of London Engineering

College, and resulted in the decision to build the front end of the locomotive in the form of a horizontal wedge. The original intention, as has been revealed by Mr. B. Spencer in his paper to the Institution of Locomotive Engineers, to which I have referred previously, was to provide a casing level on top from the chimney back to the cab. But the experiments showed that, while in a head wind this plan would work, in a side wind the increased wind pressure on the windward side of the boiler and the reduced pressure on the lee side would tend to draw the exhaust down and obscure the driver's view.

Additional trials led to the evolution of the now familiar rimless chimney, pear-shaped in plan, projecting well above the sloping smokebox front at the front corner, and then curved downwards to merge with the boiler top at the point of the pear. Further assistance in smoke-lifting was given by louvres in each side of the chimney. No modification of this arrangement has ever been needed, and it has proved completely effective in service at all speeds, except with the double-chimney "A4s," mentioned later, which have given some trouble with drifting exhaust when running with short cut-offs.

Experiments next were conducted, at the National Physical Laboratory, with scale models of the proposed "A4" and of a previous "A3" Pacific, to determine of what value the streamline casing would be in overcoming air resistance at high speed. These showed a reduction to about 58 per cent., with the streamline casing, of the horsepower required to move the locomotive at all speeds from 60 to 150 m.p.h. The 150 m.p.h. speed was to simulate the effect of a locomotive running at high speed into a strong headwind. The actual horsepower economies calculated from these experiments, in favour of the streamlining, were 41 h.p. at 60 m.p.h., 97 h.p. at 80 m.p.h., 138 h.p. at 90 m.p.h., 190 h.p. at 100 m.p.h., 253 h.p. at 110 m.p.h. and 639 h.p. at 150 m.p.h.

The streamlining therefore would mean an average saving of 100 h.p. continuously on a working such as that of the "Silver Jubilee." If internal engine resistance be included, and the resistance of the train (which worked out at an average of about 620 drawbar h.p. on the London—Newcastle journey), the "A4" would have to put out an average of some 970 indicated h.p. as compared with the 1,070 h.p. of an "A3." As the average coal consumption of the "A4" Pacifics on the "Silver Jubilee" workings was found by experience to be 37·6 lb. to the mile, the streamlining therefore was worth all but 4 lb. of coal a mile, equivalent to 200 tons a year on this one train. Such a saving alone should justify any increased maintenance costs due to enclosure of the boiler and motion inside the streamline casing.

While the view of an "A4" from the dead head-on position, with the flat face of the wedge front narrowing down to the buffer-beam, was the least attractive feature of the engine's appearance, the side elevation was one of the most beautiful and shapely examples of locomotive streamlining that the world has yet seen. With the bold upward curve of the smokebox and boiler top, merging into the pointed front of the cab, and the aerofoil curve above the cylinders and motion and their valance below, the engines have always looked as though they had been built for speed.

After Gresley's death, his successor, on the ground that the valances interfered with access to the motion, had them all cut away, through the whole series of the "A4" Pacifics, and the engines have never looked quite so attractive since. As suggested in the previous paragraph, a penalty of streamlining is that the casing hides away much that must be seen in the course of day-to-day maintenance, so that a nice balance must be kept between what is gained in reduced resistance and enhanced appearance and what may be lost by the cost of stripping the casing in order to inspect what lies beneath.

Next we come to the internal modifications of the "A3" design that were made in the "A4." Most important, of course, was the raising of the working pressure from 220 to 250 lb. per sq. in. In the boiler barrel, the distance between tubeplates was reduced from 19 ft. to 18 ft., which increased the length of the firebox combustion chamber by 12 in. Very careful attention was paid to the size and shape of the steam and exhaust passages—a lesson that had been learned from the Chapelon researches in France—and care was taken, too, in the building of the engines to see that the interior of all these passages was left with a perfectly smooth surface, the aim being to give the steam as smooth and easy a passage as possible from the regulator to its final ejection from the blast-pipe.

The fruit of such careful work is readily visible to any traveller on the footplate of an "A4" who, with the help of the steam-chest pressure gauge that Gresley fitted to all these engines, will observe that when the regulator is fully opened, the steam-chest pressure and boiler pressure are almost identical. None of the pressure has been lost by frictional resistance on the way down to the cylinders.

Next, and as a part result, no doubt, of experience with *Lemberg*—which, as noted in Chapter 4, had her cylinders lined up to $18\frac{1}{4}$ in. diameter when she was fitted with a 220 lb. boiler in 1927, and thereafter became noted for her sustained high speed propensities—Gresley reduced the 19 in. cylinder diameter of the "A3" engines to $18\frac{1}{2}$ in. in the "A4." The extra space so obtained permitted an increase in the piston-valve diameter from 8 in. to 9 in., so that at last an ideal balance for maximum ease of steam-flow had been obtained between cylinders and valves. In tractive effort, the reduction in cylinder diameter was more than balanced by the increase of boiler pressure, and the 32,910 lb. of the "A3" thus was increased to 35,455 lb. tractive effort in the "A4." The standard "A3" valve-motion was fitted, with the usual conjugated arrangement for the middle valve, and maximum cut-off still limited to 65 per cent.

It is of interest to mention here that in view of the tremendous popularity of the streamline trains, from which it was nothing unusual to have to exclude passengers because all the seats had been taken, Gresley realised that a demand for longer trains eventually would become irresistible. Before his death he had designed an improved "A4" in which the working pressure would have been raised from 250 to 275 lb., and the tractive effort from 35,455 to 39,040 lb., and there was every likelihood both that this and a very powerful 6 ft. 8 in. 4-8-2 locomotive with 21 in. × 26 in. cylinders, 250 lb. pressure, 45,700 lb. tractive effort and an estimated weight of 115 tons, for which designs also were complete, would have been built. But the Second World War came;

and before it had ended the direction of L.N.E.R. locomotive affairs had passed into other hands, so that these bold ideas never came to fruition.

Another matter of great importance which came under consideration during the evolution of the "A4" design was the stability of the engines at the high speeds contemplated with the streamline trains. It had been calculated that the centre of gravity of an "A3" Pacific, in full running order, was 5 ft. $11\frac{1}{4}$ in. above rail, and this was verified, with remarkable exactitude, in a test which was carried out at Doncaster Works with No. 2598 *Blenheim*. By seizing the engine with the works cranes, and tipping her up sideways, it was proved that the calculation was no more than $\frac{1}{16}$-in. out; in working order the centre of gravity was 5 ft. $11\frac{3}{16}$ in. above the rail level, and empty 5 ft. $7\frac{7}{8}$ in. above. The centre-line of the "A4" boiler, as with all the Gresley 2-6-2, 4-6-2 and 2-8-2 designs, was pitched 9 ft. $4\frac{1}{2}$ in. above rail level.

It was also necessary to pay close attention to the way in which the "A4" engines would hold the track at high speed. Originally the springs which control the lateral sliding movement of the bogie were designed to exert a force of 2 tons when first brought into action, and a maximum of $4\frac{1}{2}$ tons when the full lateral displacement of 4 in. was reached. But after the streamline trains had come into service, it was found that the flanges of the leading pair of coupled wheels were wearing more rapidly than those of the middle and trailing pair, and to correct this tendency the initial force of the bogie control springs was altered to 4 tons, and the maximum to 7 tons. At the same time an alteration was made to the slides controlling the action of the radial wheels at the rear end of the engine: to reduce their control, their inclination was modified from 1 in 7 to 1 in $10\frac{2}{3}$. The combined alteration was found to be effective.

In balancing his "A4" engines, Gresley, as with all his three-cylinder locomotives, adopted a method which in some quarters has been criticised. With most designers it is customary to distribute the balance of the reciprocating masses of both inside and outside cylinders, up to something like 40 per cent. of their weight, equally between all the coupled wheels. But Gresley, while increasing his outside cylinder balance to 60 per cent. with the "A1" Pacifics, provided balance for the inside cylinder on the driving wheels only. In the "A4" Pacifics, however, the outside cylinder balance was reduced to the more normal 40 per cent., though inside cylinder balance still remained concentrated on the driving wheels.

Mr. Spencer, in replying to the discussion following his paper on Gresley's locomotive designs (to which several previous references have been made), remarked that while this disproportion might result in the axle hammer-blow on the driving wheels being in a direction opposite to that from the leading and trailing coupled wheels, a considerable reduction was effected by this means in the whole engine hammer-blow. This arrangement had not resulted in excessive wear of crank-pins or bushes, though those responsible for track maintenance might possibly complain of the excessive hammer-blow from individual axles, which could have an adverse effect on the rail-bearers and cross-girders of bridges.

To ensure smooth riding of the "A4" Pacifics at speed, Gresley increased the distance between the hangers of the laminated springs of the driving wheels from 3 ft. 6 in. to 4 ft., and their potential deflection—the measure of their flexibility—from 0·135 in. to 0·270 in. per ton of imposed weight. The flexibility, that is to say, was doubled. It would be generally agreed that the riding qualities of an "A4" at speed are superb.

After having experimented in the matter with "A1" Pacific No. 4473 *Solario*, Gresley decided to fit the spacious cabs of the "A4s" with bucket seats for the crew, facing forwards in such a position that there would be an excellent look-out ahead from the sitting position. Though common enough in the United States, the provision of seats in the cab was a novelty for Great Britain. For accurate observance of speed restrictions, each engine was provided with a Flaman speed indicator of the self-recording type; this contains a moving tape on which the speed of the journey is recorded continuously, and keeps the speed round curves and past other speed-restricted points under official observation. The only convenient location for this bulky fitting was under the fireman's seat, where, however, the speed dial was easily visible to the driver. The cab itself was of a "wind-cutter" type, with pointed front, better adapted to aid in reducing air resistance than the flat-fronted cab of an "A1" or "A3."

As with Gresley's "P2" 2-8-2 locomotives, the only possible location for the whistle was ahead of the chimney—an interesting detail which, with the bucket seats for the crew, attracted much closer attention from the Press than any parts of the engine more intimately concerned with its ability to move a load at high speed. A chime whistle was fitted, and its beautiful tone contrasted strongly with the high-pitched note of the standard L.N.E.R. whistle. The whistle also derived from the "P2" 2-8-2s, and resulted from a visit paid by Gresley to his friend Captain Howey and to the latter's Romney, Hythe & Dymchurch Railway. Sir Nigel was so impressed with two standard Canadian Pacific whistles about to be fitted to the model C.P.R. Pacifics *Dr. Syn* and *Black Prince* that Howey presented him with one of them, to be used on one of the new L.N.E.R. 2-8-2 engines. The "A4" whistles are a more melodious version of this type. In addition, one of the later " A4s," No. 4489 *Dominion of Canada*, was presented by the Canadian Pacific Railway with a standard bell, which she still carries mounted on her sloping front below the chimney.

Lastly, it was necessary to ensure adequate brake-power for high speed running. As compared with the "A3" Pacifics, therefore, Gresley increased the brake-power of the "A4" engines from 66 to 93 per cent. of the adhesion weight, and on the tender from 53 to 62 per cent. of the weight in full running order. Nevertheless, even this modification was not sufficient to cope with the problem of pulling the "Silver Jubilee" up from a full 90 m.p.h. to a dead stand between any two of the two-aspect colour-light signals on the North Eastern Area north of York, and it is interesting to recall that this fact was responsible, indirectly, for the amazing speed of the "Silver Jubilee" trial trip which is described in the next chapter. Still more interesting, in the same connection, is the fact that it was a series of brake trials, in the year 1938, arranged to test out a quick-acting brake system which would give further protection to high speed trains, that gave the opportunity for *Mallard's* world record speed of 126 m.p.h.

The engine last-mentioned was one of the only five Pacifics to which Gresley fitted the Kylchap exhaust, with its double blast-pipe, concentric petticoats, and double chimney. The first experiments were made with "A3" Pacific No. 2751 *Humorist*, which suffered a series of most peculiar smokebox and chimney modifications, all more or less unsightly, before the present smoke-deflection arrangements on this engine were settled. No. 4468 *Mallard* was the first "A4" Pacific to be built with the double chimney, and was followed by the last three of the 34 "A4" Pacifics that Gresley built— Nos. 4901 *Capercaillie* (later renamed *Sir Charles Newton*), 4902 *Seagull*, and 4903 *Peregrine* (later renamed *Lord Faringdon*). The three engines concerned are now Nos. 60005, 60033 and 60034 in the British Railways stock, and *Mallard* has become No. 60022.

Apart from *Mallard's* epoch-making feat of speed, it is significant that in the 1948 locomotive exchange trials, out of all the "A4" Pacifics available, the double-chimney Nos. 60022, 60033 and 60034 were the three selected to represent the Eastern Region. Indeed, the performance of the double-chimney engines always has been so markedly superior to that of the remaining "A4s" as to excite surprise that no attempt has ever been made to rebuild any of the earlier "A4" engines with this valuable aid to freedom of exhaust and improved draught.

A year after the "Silver Jubilee" had entered service, in view of the highly successful working of the "A4" engines the building of fourteen more of this type was put in hand, and the first of them, No. 4482 *Golden Eagle* and No. 4483 *Kingfisher*, appeared late in 1936. A certain number of these would be needed for the additional streamlined trains between London and Edinburgh and London and the West Riding of Yorkshire, as described in the next chapter, but it was also intended to use the engines interchangeably with the "A1" and "A3" Pacifics on the principal non-streamlined main line services. Eventually the order was increased, and from 1936 to 1938 31 additional "A4s" were turned out of Doncaster Works, bringing the total up to 35.

The numbering was on curiously casual lines. Following on the original "Silver Jubilee" engines, Nos. 2509 to 2512 inclusive, came Nos. 4482 to 4498. But before Nos. 4499 and 4500 were built, Nos. 4462 to 4469 were interposed; and finally there came another short series, completely isolated in numbers, from 4900 to 4903 inclusive. This was in accordance with L.N.E.R. numbering practice at that time, however, blocks of numbers being allocated as they became available when new engines were under construction, in sequence only when sequence was possible without re-numbering of existing engines.

When No. 4498 had been completed, at the end of 1937, the one-hundredth Gresley Pacific had come into being. By the express desire of the directors, this auspicious occasion was signalised by naming the engine *Sir Nigel Gresley*—a well-deserved tribute to the fine work that this distinguished engineer had done for his company, and a recognition of the high level to which his designing enterprise had raised London & North Eastern prestige. The naming ceremony took place at Marylebone terminus on November 26th, 1937. It is not inappropriate that No. 4498 has always been one of the most capable performers of the entire "A4" series.

The building of the last "A4" in 1938, No. 4903 *Peregrine*, later renamed *Lord Faringdon*, completed the list of the Gresley Pacifics built during the designer's lifetime, 114 all told. Of these all are still in active service with one exception, No. 4469. This engine, first named *Gadwall* and then renamed *Sir Ralph Wedgwood*, was unfortunate enough to catch the full force of a German bomb at York on the night of April 29th, 1942, and was so badly damaged as to be incapable of repair. The remains of the engine were therefore broken up, and the name was transferred to No. 4466, which until then had been *Herring Gull*.

Having recalled the introduction of the "A4" Pacifics, and examined in detail the design, we must now review some of the outstanding performances of these remarkable engines, more especially on the trial runs which preceded the introduction of the streamline trains, as well as the average quality of performance demanded by these high speed schedules.

7

The "Silver Jubilee"

September 27th, 1935, is a day which will remain firmly imprinted on my memory for as long as I live. The new "Silver Jubilee", Britain's first streamline train, was to make her first public appearance. Three days before the stream-liner entered regular service, on September 30th, a special run to Grantham and back had been arranged, in which a large and representative company, including L.N.E.R. directors and officers, their numerous guests, and the repre-sentatives of the Press, was to participate. To me fell the task of taking the official times of the run, and I little realised what a responsibility was to fall on my shoulders!

Round about 2 p.m. we assembled on No. 6 platform at King's Cross, where the new train was drawn up, the cynosure of all eyes. Nothing like this startling vision of silver grey and stainless steel had ever been seen on British rails before. Three articulated sets made up the formation—a triplet restaurant car set in the centre, flanked by third and first-class brake "twins," with the first class at the rear. Flush windows and coach panelling, with the valances extending down between the bogies and the flexible sheets joining coach-end to coach-end, provided a completely smooth surface from one end of the train to the other. At the head stood *Silver Link*, with her striking wedge front and revolutionary outline.

As the scheduled departure time of 2.25 approached, we took our places in the train. Directors and their friends withdrew to the seclusion of the first class at the rear, where they were destined to appreciate to the full all the extreme possibilities of "tail swing" at high speed. I ensconced myself in a facing corner of a compartment in the leading third class brake, where I hoped to be able to work without disturbance. On the engine were Driver Arthur Taylor and Fireman Luty, who were about to make locomotive history.

Accompanying them was Mr. I. S. W. Groom, Locomotive Running Superintendent of the Southern Area.

Prompt to time at 2.25 we started, amid the cheers of an enormous crowd assembled on No. 10 platform. At this stage it should be remarked that although the point-to-point times of the schedule laid down for the special were those calculated for the regular "Silver Jubilee" working from the following Monday, it was the intention to use the trial trip for the purpose of ascertaining what power the engine had in reserve. As mentioned in the previous chapter, at the last minute it had been realised that the brake-power of engine and train was insufficient to pull the "Silver Jubilee" up from 90 m.p.h. to a dead stop between any one of the North Eastern Area colour-light signals north of York and the next, should the line not be clear, For this reason it would now be necessary to restrict the maximum speed between York and Darlington to 70 m.p.h., and to cut the schedule south of York in order to compensate for the minutes lost in this way. So *Silver Link* was to be "given her head" on this run.

It was not long before this determination became apparent. By Wood Green we were up to 70 m.p.h., and from there, instead of dropping in speed up the long 1 in 200 to Potter's Bar, the engine accelerated steadily with her 230-ton load, until we topped the summit at 75! Then, accelerating like lightning past Marsh Moor and Red Hall, we added another 20 to sweep through Hatfield at all but 95, and touched 98 at the point where the railway crosses the River Lea.

It was at the London end of Hatfield down platform, over a trailing connection from a siding, that there came the first of a series of alarming shocks that were to make this journey one of the most unnerving of my life. Gresley had devised a special system of suspension for his new stock which would cause the coach-bodies to "float" at high speed, but, like the bogie side-control springs of the locomotive, the springs controlling lateral movement of the coach bogies also were too flexible. So when, for track reasons explained in the next paragraph, centrifugal force caused the coach-bodies to make a lateral movement of any amplitude, the effect was suddenly to compress these springs to the limit, imparting a jerk to the coach-body that at times was quite unnerving. The Press representatives regarded these sensations, no doubt, as a satisfying proof that we were travelling fast; but on those of us "in the know" the effect was rather different!

The track conditions to which I have referred were these. It would not be disputed that maintenance of the old Great Northern main line in general was of a high standard. But so far as this new service was concerned, it can hardly be claimed that *liaison* between the Mechanical, Operating and Civil Engineering Departments had been of the best. Both from the experimental runs of the previous November and March and from the schedule laid down for the "Silver Jubilee," it must have been obvious to the civil engineering authorities what speeds would be necessary to keep time. Yet little or nothing had been done to adapt the track to regular speeds far higher than ever contemplated previously.

In general, the curves were canted for a maximum speed of 70 m.p.h., and were reasonably comfortable at 80 to 85, which until then was rarely exceeded. The "transitioning" of curves—that is, the laying in of a spiral entry and exit, with a gradual working up of the cant to its full figure, in place of the previous direct tangenting—was in but an early stage of development. Thus the most violent shocks that we experienced on this hectic journey were from curves over which the cant was deficient at such speeds, or, through lack of transition, was too suddenly attained or lost. In this way we suffered two tremendous "biffs" through Hatfield, one at the station, and another at a curve a little later on; the engine then tore up the 1 in 200 to Woolmer Green as though it were not there, giving us another violent shake-up as we passed at 88 m.p.h. over a curve later restricted to 70. Apparently the riding of *Silver Link* herself was admirable, and those on the engine had not the slightest idea of the sensations to which they were subjecting their passengers! But the major excitements were yet to come.

It was at the 30th milepost that the speed first crossed the "100" line. From then onwards, for 25 miles on end, *Silver Link* blazed away at this enormous speed and more. To the crowd of watchers on Hitchin platforms it must have been the sight of a lifetime as we hurled ourselves through the station at 107. By Arlesey we were up to 112½; and from here onwards the engine was demonstrating her ability to keep up a steady 105 or so on little easier than level track. Indeed, at St. Neot's, after climbing 3¾ miles at 1 in 330 (with a short downhill break in the middle of it) we were still doing 104½ an hour!

By now there had drifted into my compartment Sir Nigel himself, completely imperturbable, armed with a chronograph watch of vast dimensions which he had had made specially for speed recording purposes. He sat down next to me, and beyond him Mr. Chas. J. Brown, Chief Civil Engineer, under whom I was serving at that time ; the latter was a nervous man, and his face betrayed the fact by being some shades paler than normally. On the opposite seat sat

TABLE 2.

The "Silver Jubilee" Trial Trip

September 27th, 1935
Engine, "A4" 4-6-2 No. 2509 *Silver Link*
Load, 220 tons tare, 230 tons full

Dist.		Sched.	Actual	Speeds
miles		min.	min. sec.	m.p.h.
0·0	KING'S CROSS	0	0 00	—
2·5	Finsbury Park	—	4 42	—
5·0	Wood Green	—	7 11	70
9·2	New Barnet	—	10 43	72
12·7	Potters Bar	—	13 36	75
17·7	HATFIELD	18½	17 07	94½
20·3	Welwyn Garden City	—	18 46	98
23·5	Woolmer Green	—	20 52	88
25·0	Knebworth	—	21 55	‡93½
28·6	Stevenage	—	24 13	90
30·0	Milepost 30	—	25 06	100
31·9	HITCHIN	29½	26 14	107
37·0	Arlesey	—	29 03	112½
41·1	Biggleswade	—	31 22	§105
44·1	Sandy	—	32 59	112½
47·5	Tempsford	—	34 50	109½
51·7	St. Neot's	—	37 13	104½
55·0	Milepost 55	—	39 03	109½
56·0	Offord	—	39 41	*85
58·9	HUNTINGDON	48½	41 41	88
62·0	Milepost 62	—	43 53	83½
63·5	Abbot's Ripton	—	44 58	—
69·4	Holme	—	48 50	93½
72·6	Yaxley	—	51 08	80½
75·0	Fletton Junction	—	52 55	—
76·4	PETERBOROUGH	†63½	†55 02	*20

* Speed restriction. † Passing time.
‡ At Langley Junction. § At Langford.

Mr. Randolph Churchill, collecting impressions of the run for the *Daily Mail*, and in search of some facts about the speed. With every fresh lurch of our coach, the Chief Mechanical Engineer directed shafts of wit at the Chief Civil Engineer concerning the condition of the latter's track, not altogether appreciated by the recipient!

THE GRESLEY PACIFICS OF THE L.N.E.R.

Between deference to these distinguished visitors, anxiety to concentrate on the all-important business of recording accurately the run of a century, and speculation as to whether, at all but 110 m.p.h., some one-and-one-eighth inches of steel flange would suffice to hold us to the rails on the sinuous Offord curves now dead ahead, or whether we should dive straight into the River Ouse, the state of my mind can be better imagined than described!

However, Driver Taylor showed sufficient regard for Offord to touch down to 85, over curves later restricted permanently to a maximum of 70! By now the most staggering part of the journey was over. Shall we ever repeat such times, I wonder? Nine minutes, seven seconds from Hatfield to Hitchin; fifteen minutes seventeen seconds over the 27·0 miles from Hitchin to Huntingdon! From Hatfield to Huntingdon, 41·2 miles, we had averaged 100·6 m.p.h. throughout; between mileposts 30 and 55, where the speed had never fallen below 100, the average had been 107·5 m.p.h. and for 43 miles on end an average of 100 m.p.h. had been kept up. So it was that *Silver Link* rolled under the footbridge at the centre of Peterborough North station *fifty-five minutes after leaving King's Cross* (*plus* a paltry two seconds).

Having recovered from a 20 m.p.h. slack through Peterborough to 83 m.p.h. again by Essendine, we stood a good chance of reaching Grantham in 80 minutes from London, but adverse signals were now sighted. We had caught up the 1.40 p.m. express from King's Cross, which had left 45 minutes ahead of us! Finally, we stopped at Grantham in 88 min. 15 sec. from London. The excitement was over; although there was some very fast running in places, including a time of 20 min. 12 sec. for the 27·0 miles from Huntingdon to Hitchin, and a top speed of 94 m.p.h. at Tempsford, nothing of the extreme order of the down run was attempted on the way back. But the effect on my nerves had been such that when I was asked to go down to Newcastle on the first public run of the "Silver Jubilee," three days later, to record the times for Press purposes, I found a convenient excuse of urgent work elsewhere; a repetition of our hectic inaugural experiences, with darkness added over much of the journey, seemed beyond the limit of human endurance!

THE
STREAM-
LINERS

(*Above*) "A4" No. 2509 *Silver Link* in original silver-grey livery and with painted-on name.

(*Below*) "A4" No. 2512 *Silver Fox* climbs past Abbots Ripton with the up "Silver Jubilee."

[*British Railways, C. C. B. Herbert*

(Above) THE TWO 4 O'CLOCKS — The down "Coronation," headed by No. 4466 *Herring Gull* (now *Sir Ralph Wedgwood*), pulls away from 4-6-4 No. 10000 between the tunnels north of King's Cross.

(*Left*) DECORATION — "A4" No. 4489 *Dominion of Canada*, with the bell presented by the Canadian Pacific Railway.

[*Photos.: C. C. B. Herbert*

(Right)

SERVICING — "A4" No. 2509 *Silver Link* at King's Cross between arrival and departure with the "Silver Jubilee." Note handle in position by the cylinder for opening up the wedge front to get at the smokebox door.

(Below)

THE "WEST RIDING LIMITED" — "A4" No. 4496 *Golden Shuttle* with the up train near Potters Bar Tunnel.

[*P. Ransome-Wallis, C. C. B. Herbert*

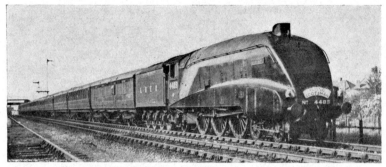

[*P. Ransome-Wallis*

"A4" IN GREEN LIVERY—No. 4485 *Kestrel*, one of the "A4s" which appeared in 1936 for ordinary service, heads the up "Flying Scotsman" past Potters Bar.

!N EMERGENCIES, "A1" and "A3" Pacifics were occasionally seen on the streamline trains "A1" No. 2570 *Tranquil* passes Low Fell with the down "Coronation" in June, 1938.

[*W. B. Greenfield*

[*F. R. Hebron*

THE 1948 EXCHANGES—"A4" No. 60034 *Lord Faringdon* climbs Camden Bank with the down L.M.R. "Royal Scot." Note the cut-away valances above the wheels and motion.

After this, Gresley lost no time in modifying the spring suspension of the stock, and the Chief Civil Engineer at last took a revision of the track levels seriously in hand, laying down numerous slight speed restrictions—70 or 80 m.p.h.—at points where the track could not be improved sufficiently to permit a maximum of 90 m.p.h. Seeing that both these officers, together with the directors and their guests, experienced to the full all the startling sensations of the trial trip, it could hardly be otherwise!

With this attention the riding of the "Silver Jubilee" soon settled down to something quite reasonably steady. " Nevertheless," as I wrote later in *The Railway Magazine*, " this and the other L.N.E.R. streamliners always had their exciting moments, especially when they were newly out of the shops after overhaul and particularly lively on their springing in consequence. Removal by the staff of the vases of flowers from the restaurant car tables, as the 'Jubilee' forged its way through the tunnels from King's Cross, was on such occasions a solemn ritual resembling the ceremony of putting the fiddles on the dining saloon tables at sea. Yet, as we pursued our uneasy course through dinner, the only nonchalant comment from Teesside or Tyneside *habitués* in the opposite pew—for the ever-popular 'Silver Bullet.' as they called it, always had the atmosphere, at its first-class end, of a travelling club—would be 'It's a rough night to-night,' or words to that effect, and their appetites would not appear to be in the least impaired." Generally, however, one could depend on a smooth and comfortable trip, though certain specific points, such as Shaftholme Junction, had their special liveliness which was better in retrospect than in prospect!

Seldom, if ever, before has a train swung into such immediate popularity as the "Silver Jubilee." From the very start it ran filled to capacity day after day, and passengers who had not booked their seats well in advance stood the risk of not getting on the streamliner at all. North East Coast business men appreciated to the full the advantage of being able to go to their offices and see their letters, then board the train at Newcastle at 10 a.m., or its connection from Middlesbrough at the same hour, be whisked into King's Cross by 2 p.m. for an afternoon engagement in the capital, start back after $3\frac{1}{2}$ hours at 5.30 p.m., and be in their home stations once again by 9.30 p.m. Moreover, these times could be relied on, for despite the almost entire novelty of a schedule at such speeds, keen engine-crews took to the idea at once, and timekeeping was exemplary.

Between King's Cross and Darlington the allowance in each direction for the 232·3 miles was 198 minutes. Some of the point-to-point timings were extremely fast, in particular the 19 minutes allowed for the 27·0 miles from Hitchin to Huntingdon, which demanded an *average* speed of 85·3 m.p.h. over this length. On the down journey the "Jubilee" was booked through Peterborough, 76·4 miles, in $63\frac{1}{2}$ minutes, Grantham, 105·5 miles, in $87\frac{1}{2}$ minutes, and York, 188·2 miles, in $157\frac{1}{2}$ minutes. Later on, these times were slightly eased, after the substitution of three-aspect for two-aspect colour-light signalling north of York had made it possible to increase the maximum speed over that magnificent racing-ground from 70 to the normal 90 m.p.h. of the remainder of the route.

In view of the cut of over an hour in the best previous times between London and Newcastle, a small supplementary fare of 5s. first class and 3s. third class was exacted for the privilege of using the train, but it was soon demonstrated that the public had no objection whatever to paying on this modest scale for the privilege of high speed. The "Silver Jubilee" regularly was earning gross receipts of about 14s. a mile, every day that it ran, and in two years the supplements alone paid the entire cost of building the rolling stock.

Moreover, so far from high speed in itself being dangerous— notwithstanding the terrifying discomforts of the trial trip!— during the four years that the " Silver Jubilee " ran, up to the outbreak of war in 1939, it was never involved in any major mishap. Indeed, between September 30th, 1935, and October 9th, 1937, the "Silver Jubilee" set of coaches covered in all 277,370 miles, of which 230,200 miles were at a booked average of 70·4 m.p.h., and 162,030 miles at 75 m.p.h., and once only during this period was the train held up by a hot box. Saturdays and Sundays, with the Christmas and Easter holiday periods, gave ample time for maintenance; but even so, this was a very fine record. As previously mentioned, the speed "ceiling" was fixed at 90 m.p.h., and in normal running, with the watchdog provided by the Flaman speed indicators and their continuous recording tapes, drivers seldom much exceeded these figures. But every now and again one would clock a "100," especially if the speed indicator happened to be out of order, and there was a speed merchant at the front end!

The second of the streamlined 4-6-2s, No. 2510 *Quicksilver*, was not ready to take a share in the working of the "Silver Jubilee" until the third week after the service had started. There soon followed No. 2511 *Silver King* and No. 2512 *Silver Fox*. The last-mentioned was presented by the United Steel Companies with stainless steel representations of a fox in full flight, made at their Samuel Fox steelworks at Stocksbridge, which were fixed to both sides of the boiler casing, as well as stainless steel clothing bands and hand-rails to the boiler; these the engine still carries. This engine was destined to earn notoriety in the following year by a high speed exploit which had an unforeseen aftermath, as described later.

Silver King was stationed at Gateshead as a reserve engine, and spent most of her time running between Newcastle and Edinburgh. At week-ends, when the "Silver Jubilee" did not run on Saturdays and Sundays, the other three "A4s" soon began to be drafted to heavy regular workings, such as the " Flying Scotsman," and so to prove a measure of competence in such service no whit inferior to their work on the high speed lightweight train.

Precisely eleven months after the historic "Silver Jubilee" trial trip, on August 27th, 1936, it was decided to make a run from Newcastle to King's Cross with the dynamometer car added to the seven-car "Jubilee" set. This brought the weight for the first time up to 254 tare tons, or 270 tons including the passenger complement. It was the official intention to do something out of the ordinary down the long descent southwards from Stoke, and representatives of *The Times* and other papers were invited to be in attendance at King's Cross on our arrival in order to obtain "hot news" of what had happened. I was permitted to join the staff in the dynamometer car, and this was another occasion that I am never likely to forget.

The train ran normally as far as Grantham. The driver was Haygreen of King's Cross, and his work at the regulator was not very impressive; there was very little of the full regulator, and much of the engine's work was being done with 130 to 180 lb. pressure in the steam-chest out of the rated 250 lb. Even up the hills the regulator was not opened more than to give 200 to 220 lb. or so at the pistons.

At last, at Grantham, the regulator was opened to full. But now the boiler pressure itself was only 215 to 225 lb., so that with 25 per cent. cut-off we fell from $71\frac{1}{2}$ to $68\frac{1}{2}$ m.p.h. on the 1 in 200 up to Stoke. Once over the summit Haygreen notched up to 15 per cent., but then had gradually to open out to 25, 30, and finally 35 per cent. to reach the 113 m.p.h. which eventually was touched, not on the 1 in 200 past Little Bytham, where speed had flattened out to 106, but on the easier strips of level and 1 in 264 down after Essendine. Had the boiler pressure been up to the full 250 lb. at Stoke, we could have reached the same speed and more without having to flog the engine to an extent that was to have unfortunate results.

It was after we had passed Peterborough that a very slight periodic irregularity began to show itself in the drawbar pull curve on the dynamometer car roll. Nothing untoward happened, however, until we had roared through Hatfield at about 85 m.p.h.; to this point we had taken 177 min. 52 sec. for the 214·4 miles from Darlington, and were about 4 minutes ahead of time. Suddenly a rain of fragments hit the underside of the dynamometer car, with little doubt stone ballast thrown up by something which had dropped from the engine. Speed began to fall, and an anxious colloquy as to what had happened started over the "inter-com." between car and footplate, punctuated by one or two further bombardments from below.

Nevertheless it was decided to proceed; and the next twenty-four minutes were among the most nerve-racking that several of us at the front end had ever spent. Speed gradually dropped; there had been a sharp reduction at Brookman's Park, and for most of the distance down from Potter's Bar we ran without steam. It had to be put on again to get into the platform at King's Cross, and with *Silver Fox* roaring like a wounded bull, and steam shooting straight out at the front end, we dragged our way up the platform finally to come to rest a bare seven minutes late.

It was found that the middle big-end bearing metal had melted; the big-end itself, with additional play, had disintegrated completely; both cylinder-ends had been pushed off; and it is a miracle indeed that we escaped a much more serious casualty, if not disaster. A train-load of passengers, some of them taking lunch at the time, had been moved at the highest speed ever attained by a British passenger train in ordinary service—a record which still holds—but we had had a reminder that very high speeds are not unattended by risk.

Notwithstanding these excitements, it was decided to carry on with the return dynamometer trip that day as planned, and for this *Silver Link* was assigned, in charge of Bill Sparshatt. Our late friend had been solemnly warned that there were to be no fireworks, and his observance, whether of the overriding speed limit of 90 m.p.h. south of York and 70 m.p.h. beyond, or of all service slacks, was meticulous in the extreme. But the engine was handled to perfection, and inclusive of all slacks he ran the 160·3 miles from Potter's Bar to Brayton Junction, Selby, at an average of 77·2 m.p.h.

From the start the full 65 per cent. cut-off was in use, reduced to 45 per cent. by Holloway and 25 per cent. at Finsbury Park, which Sparshatt continued to use as far as Potter's Bar, as steam pressure was down to 205 lb. along this stage. After that 18 per cent. was the cut-off generally in use, and at this figure, with full regulator, and a pressure of 230-235 lb. in the steam-chest when the boiler pressure was at 235-240 lb.—again a tribute to the design and layout of the steam passages—the uphill work was grand, especially when we attained 90 m.p.h. with 270 tons up the 1 in 440 beyond Tallington, climbed 1¾ miles at 1 in 264 at a minimum of 86½, reached 88 again on the easier stretch beyond, mounted 4½ miles of 1 in 200 at a minimum of 78½, and finally, after re-attaining 80½ on the easy 1½ miles past Corby, carried the final 3 miles at 1 in 178 by storm at a minimum of 75 m.p.h. This gave us the wonderful average of 82·6 m.p.h., with 270 tons of train, for the whole of the 15·3 miles from Tallington up to Stoke! Times and speeds of this run as far as York are set out in detail in Table 3, Chapter 9. Finally we reached Darlington in 194 min. 43 sec. from London (232·3 miles), and Newcastle 4 minutes early at 9·26 p.m., another feather in the cap of *Silver Link*, pioneer engine of the "A4" series.

8

126 Miles per Hour

Streamline service having proved so extremely popular with the public, the London & North Eastern management, probably not without stimulus from Gresley, began to look around for fresh fields to conquer. Just as the "Silver Jubilee" had been so named in order to commemorate the fruitful twenty-five years of the reign of King George V, it was decided to mark the year of coronation of King George VI by the introduction of a second streamline train called "Coronation." This would run at such a time as to provide Tyneside with an evening flight to London in addition to the morning "Silver Jubilee." But the main purpose was to bring the capitals of England and Scotland, London and Edinburgh, within the unprecedented time of 6 hours of one another daily, and, moreover, to give patrons of the train up to the late afternoon of the day—4 p.m. in London and 4.30 p.m. in Edinburgh—before having to start their journeys.

The working of the "Silver Jubilee" had provided all the information needed for the London-Newcastle stage of the run. To obtain some useful data for the Newcastle-Edinburgh stage, a special train of 252 tons' weight, dynamometer car included, was run from Newcastle to Edinburgh and back on Saturday, September 26th, 1936, with "A4" 4-6-2 No. 2511 *Silver King*. Driver Dron made the northbound run of 124·4 miles in 118 minutes and the return journey in 114 minutes. Of the southbound trip a grand effort was the ascent of the 4 miles at 1 in 96 of Cockburnspath bank, which was topped at the remarkable speed of 68 m.p.h. This required a drawbar h.p. of 1,460 and an indicated h.p. of between 2,500 and 2,600. The latter, of course, was a calculated figure, for because of the streamlined casing it has never yet been possible to indicate an "A4" locomotive.

The inauguration of the "Coronation" service was timed for July, 1937. Five of the latest "A4" Pacifics were assigned to the "Coronation" train—Nos. 4488 *Union of South Africa,* 4489 *Dominion of Canada,* 4490 *Empire of India,* 4491 *Commonwealth of Australia,* and 4492 *Dominion of New Zealand*—and these were painted in a beautiful shade of Garter blue, later to become the standard for the entire "A4" series, with stainless steel numbers, letters and mouldings. Nos. 4488 and 4489 at first were named *Osprey* and *Woodcock* respectively, before the "Dominion" series of names was decided on. No. 4489 first appeared in grey, but was painted blue a few weeks later when renamed.

When the two new "Coronation" trains appeared, competent observers were astonished indeed at the task which Gresley proposed to set his "A4" Pacifics in hauling them. For whereas he had restricted the weight of the "Silver Jubilee" to a seven-coach formation of 220 tare tons, the "Coronation" sets were of nine vehicles each, four twin articulated sets with an observation car of novel design at the rear end. Apart from the two additional vehicles, the provision of two separate kitchen cars and of electrically-operated air-conditioning throughout each train helped to put the total tare load up to 312 tons—42 per cent. more than that of the "Silver Jubilee." Moreover, the "Coronation" was to be worked to York, 188·2 miles from King's Cross, in no more than 157 minutes, at an average of 71·9 m.p.h.—the fastest schedule ever to appear in a British time-table.

At first York was the only stop on the down journey, but Newcastle was too important to be omitted, and later on a stop at Newcastle was made also, so that the run of 392·7 miles between King's Cross and Edinburgh had to be completed in six hours with two intermediate stops of three minutes' duration each. In the up direction, Newcastle was the only halt, and the 268·3 miles from there to London were run non-stop in 3 hours, 57 minutes. In both directions, as was the general custom in those days, the work exacted of the engines south of York was considerably harder than that over the North Eastern Area—a curious reversal of the practice of both earlier and later years—so that in the event of any time being dropped to York going north, there was a good chance of recovering it before Edinburgh.

Not so coming south, however; and there were one or two

days at least of bad weather conditions when the entire contents of the coal bunker had disappeared from the tender of the Pacific working the up "Coronation" well before the end of the journey, so making necessary a stop at Hitchin for help. This was partly due to the original tender coverings of the streamlined engines; while at King's Cross shed care was taken to pack the coal into the corners under the coverings, Haymarket shed used to drop the coal on to the tenders from above, in the ordinary way, and as a result the engines might leave Edinburgh for the south without the coal space being filled to capacity. But after the unfortunate casualty at Wiske Moor, north of Northallerton, when an inspector riding on the footplate with the southbound "Coronation" was killed because of the rush of water that came over the tender top when the two streamliners met at speed on Wiske Moor troughs, the tender coverings were removed, and there was no difficulty after that in ensuring that the engines had a full coal supply.

Nevertheless, as with the "Silver Jubilee," the reliability of the "A4" Pacifics, even on so onerous an assignment as this, was wonderful. From the inauguration of the "Coronation" service, *Commonwealth of Australia* worked either the down or up train for 48 out of the first 51 days—that is, for all but three days of the first ten weeks—just as *Dominion of New Zealand* worked the non-stop "Flying Scotsman" on 52 out of the first 54 days of its running after the schedule had been pared to 7 hours. On the "Coronation" workings the average coal consumption between London and Edinburgh, in normal conditions, worked out at about 43 lb. per mile, as compared with the $37\frac{1}{2}$ lb. of the "Silver Jubilee." But the disproportion in the power demand north and south of York must have involved the engines in a considerably higher rate of consumption on the King's Cross-York stage of their journeys than over the remainder.

The two "Coronation" observation cars were interesting vehicles. At the rear end, each of them reversed the locomotive wedge front by being built in the form of a "beaver tail"—a fine piece of coach-building craftsmanship. The idea, of course, was to reduce the rear-end resistance caused by the square end of an ordinary tail-coach creating a vacuum behind it as it moves through the atmosphere at high speed. So marshalled, the "Coronation" trains were a perfect example of complete streamlining from head to tail—wedge-fronted locomotive with aerofoil curves and valances over the motion, and wedge-fronted cab; coaches with flush windows and side panels, with rubber sheeting joining coach to coach; and beaver tail.

During the first winter the "Coronation" ran, however, it was realised that with starts from the two terminals as late as 4.0 and 4.30 p.m. the opportunities of "observation" from the rear end were negligible, as nearly all the journey was being made in darkness, and the tail cars therefore were withdrawn during the winter months. By reducing the tare load to 279 tons, this gave the locomotives some welcome relief to compensate for the adverse effects of winter weather conditions. It is of interest, by the way, that experience with the relatively heavy "Coronation" formations decided Gresley to agree to provide an additional coach on the "Silver Jubilee", which invariably ran filled to capacity. So the leading brake third "twin" of the latter was rebuilt as a "triplet," bringing the number of vehicles up to eight, and the tare weight to 248 tons.

As previously with the "Silver Jubilee," the inauguration of the "Coronation" service was preceded by Press trip, which took place on June 30th. Nothing like the *tour de force* of the "Silver Jubilee" trial was attempted on the down journey; indeed, it is doubtful if such times would have been even possible with the much increased load. *Dominion of Canada* was the engine, and Driver Burfoot stuck closely to his schedule all the way to Grantham; we were a minute late through Hatfield (19 min. 29 sec.), but ¾-minute ahead at Peterborough (62 min. 50 sec.) and passed Grantham almost on the stroke of the 87½ minutes allowed (87 min. 34 sec.), reaching Barkston North, 111·1 miles (where the train was to be turned round the Barkston triangle) in 93 min. 29 sec.

But on the return journey it was decided once again to whip one of the Pacifics up to a 100 m.p.h. speed. There was some incentive, moreover, as two days earlier the London Midland & Scottish Railway claimed to have wrested the speed supremacy from the London & North Eastern by touching 114 m.p.h.

in a test run with their new "Coronation Scot" on the descent from Whitmore to Crewe, though with 270 tons of train only as compared with our 320 tons. So Burfoot started *Dominion of Canada* away from Barkston with such vigour that by Grantham we were already doing 66 m.p.h., and accelerated further to 69 up the 1 in 200 to Stoke.

Then came the lightning speed down towards Peterborough to which these various tests were by now making us almost accustomed—86½ m.p.h. by Corby, and in succession from milepost 97, miles at 90·0, 92·3, 97·3, 100·0, 102·9, 107·5 and 109·1 m.p.h. (posts 91 to 90), after which speed tailed away to 101·5 and 94·7 m.p.h. over the next two miles. The actual maximum was 109½ m.p.h., so we had failed to reach the L.M.S.R. figure by 4½ m.p.h., or even to equal the previous L.N.E.R. figure. It was a cause of acute disappointment at Doncaster that the L.M.S.R. remained unbeaten, but subsequent experience of No. 4489 showed that her performance did not equal that of the rest of the batch, so that an unhappy choice of engine had been made on this occasion. Nevertheless, in the load conditions, the failure was quite an honourable one. From Grantham to Peterborough the 29·1 miles took 20 min. 53 sec. After that we were content to stick to schedule, and ran from Grantham to King's Cross in 86 min. 3 sec., as compared with our allowance of 86½ minutes.

Once again I was asked to accompany the first regular down run of the "Coronation," on the following Monday, to take times for publicity purposes, and this time, unlike 1935, it was a pleasure to do so. *Commonwealth of Australia* was our engine, and with a full complement of passengers the gross load was about 312 tons. I have vivid recollections of this trip. The Chief Engineer of the Southern Area was a passenger, and from time to time he would rise solemnly from his pew in another part of the car to ascertain from me to what extent our driver was exceeding the precise speed limits which the Engineer's Department had now laid down.

Certainly we had some lively moments—Hatfield at 86½ m.p.h., an acceleration to 90 before Langley troughs (braked to 67 to take water), 88 through Hitchin and 94 beyond, 98 at Holme—these took us through Peterborough in 61 min. 20 sec. We were through Grantham in 85 min. 17 sec., and despite a permanent way slowing immediately after, cleared Doncaster, 156·0 miles, in the fine time of 125 min. 11 sec. from King's Cross, nearly 3½ minutes early. After that Driver Dron took things relatively easily, and we were at a stand under the great curved roof at York in 155 min. 36 sec. from London. In the first hour we had covered 75¾ miles, and in the second— allowing for the permanent way slowing—another 75½ miles, a remarkably consistent piece of high speed work. This run also appears in detail in Table 3, Chapter 9.

Nothing needs to be said about the remainder of the journey to Edinburgh other than to comment on the fact that the Engineer's Department in Scotland appeared to have learned nothing from what had happened on the "Silver Jubilee" trial two years before. Other than the few special speed restrictions, such as that through Berwick, nothing had been done to lay down any higher speed limits for curves of less severity. This fact we were to appreciate to the full going down Cockburnspath bank, for when we struck the reverse curves below Innerwick we were doing a modest 94 m.p.h.! I was travelling at the time in the "beaver tail," which wagged itself with such terrific vigour as to project luggage from a rack on one side of the car in a beautifully curved trajectory clean across to the floor on the other! Nevertheless we survived this Scottish excitement, and ran into Waverley a shade after 9·59 p.m., nicely on time.

While the "Empire" engines took the major part in working the "Coronation" streamliner, other "A4" Pacifics were drafted to it when necessary, and occasionally, in an emergency, even non-streamlined "A3s" took a share, as mentioned in the next chapter. The same happened when the "West Riding Limited," last of the three L.N.E.R. streamline trains, made its appearance at the beginning of October, 1937. The two "A4" engines specially named for and allocated to this service were No. 4495 *Golden Fleece* and 4496 *Golden Shuttle*, which, like Nos. 4488 to 4492 inclusive, received the new blue livery almost from the time of their construction (No. 4495 ran in green as *Great Snipe* for a week or so), but this train also was worked by other "A4s" from time to time.

Going down, the "West Riding Limited" was not so good a timekeeper as its two predecessors. A surprisingly late departure from King's Cross was arranged, at 7.10 p.m., which projected this flyer into the middle of the evening down fast freights; and at the end of its journey, in addition, it was on the tail of the 5.50 p.m. from King's Cross to Leeds, due in Leeds Central only ten minutes earlier and also not the best of timekeepers. The result was that signal checks were not as rare as they ought to have been. But on the up journey the "West Riding Limited" trailed the up "Silver Jubilee" at a 15-minute interval, and so could be reasonably certain of a good road. The "West Riding Limited" was an eight-car set, exactly similar to the "Coronation" other than having no observation car, and weighed 279 tons empty.

As with the previous streamliners, there was a Press trip, this time from Leeds Central down to Barkston, where we turned on the triangle, and back to Leeds. *Golden Fleece* was the engine, but as we had no lengthy incline to run down like the southward descent from Stoke, there were no very thrilling moments; the highest speed was $93\frac{1}{2}$ m.p.h. at Crow Park, going south. The only excitement was that of taking Retford level crossing, at a time well before its more recent relaying and realignment, at 75 m.p.h., which gave the party a very hearty shaking up. By now, however, many of us were getting more acclimatised to such sensations!

We come now to the most startling performance for which any Gresley locomotive ever was responsible, and it is significant, as suggested previously, that it should have been achieved by an engine equipped, not only with complete external streamlining, but also with the internal "streamlining" resulting from the improvements in the steam passages that Gresley had effected in the "A4s," and, above all, by the freedom of exhaust that the doubling of blast-pipe and chimney made possible. The engine concerned, of course, was *Mallard*, and the occasion was the memorable test run of July 7th, 1938.

The nominal reason for the 1938 trials was that experiments were in progress with a type of quick-acting vacuum brake which would make it possible to pull up the streamline trains more smartly, from the maximum speeds that they attained habitually, than the standard brakes in use. As mentioned already, this problem had a direct effect on the schedule of the

"Silver Jubilee" until the two-aspect colour-light signalling north of York had been replaced by three-aspect signals.

But there is no doubt also that the sporting instincts of Sir Nigel had been aroused by the 114 m.p.h. attained by the L.M.S.R. Pacific *Coronation* in the previous year, which had transferred the blue riband of British railway speed from the L.N.E.R. to the L.M.S.R.—a fact of which the latter company had not failed to take very adequate publicity advantage!— and that he was determined, under the cloak of these tests, to give the rivals a speed challenge which they would have little chance of beating. In *Mallard* he found a perfect instrument for his purpose, and in Driver Duddington, of Doncaster, a fearless collaborator. The test train consisted of three of the "Coronation" twin sets, *plus* the dynamometer car, seven vehicles in all weighing 240 tons. It is fortunate that the dynamometer car was in use, as its precise accuracy put the maximum speeds attained beyond the realm of doubt.

The train was started a little north of Grantham, and passed the station at a modest 24 m.p.h., with the regulator wide open, and cut-off 40 per cent. In $2\frac{1}{4}$ miles at 1 in 200 up, the train accelerated to $59\frac{3}{4}$ m.p.h.; on $1\frac{1}{2}$ miles further with cut-off eased to 30 per cent. the speed increased to 69 m.p.h.; and up the final $1\frac{1}{2}$ miles through the tunnel to Stoke box, still at 1 in 200, $74\frac{1}{2}$ m.p.h. had been reached as the summit box was passed. Due to the expert work with the shovel of Fireman Bray, the boiler continued to supply all the steam needed for an unchanged 40 per cent. as the engine swept southwards.

From milepost 100, speeds at the end of each successive mile were $87\frac{1}{2}$, $96\frac{1}{2}$, 104, 107, $111\frac{1}{2}$, 116, 119 m.p.h. (milepost 93), and then, at the ensuing half-miles, $120\frac{3}{4}$, $122\frac{1}{2}$, 123, $124\frac{1}{4}$ and finally 125 m.p.h. at milepost $90\frac{1}{4}$, while the dynamometer record for a very short distance revealed the tremendous maximum of 126 m.p.h., the figure usually quoted, and at which the 6 ft. 8 in. driving wheels were doing more than 500 revolutions a minute. All this was at 40 per cent. cut-off with full regulator, increased between mileposts $94\frac{1}{4}$ and 93 to 45 per cent. Five miles (posts 94 to 89) were reeled off at an average of 120·4 m.p.h., and speed actually exceeded 120 m.p.h. for three miles continuously (posts $92\frac{3}{4}$ to $89\frac{3}{4}$). So the record was secure; *Mallard* had travelled faster, not only than the

L.M.S.R. *Coronation*, but also than all other steam locomotives in the world whose high speed performances, properly authenticated by a sequence of passing times, are on record.

Now, once again, the price had to be paid. The over-running of the middle valve-spindle, with cut-offs as lengthy as 40 and even 45 per cent. and full regulator at such enormous speeds, was bound to have been considerable, and no middle big-end of a Gresley Pacific was likely to stand up to such a punishment. Certainly the middle big-end of *Mallard* refused to do so. But with the record in his pocket, there was no need for the driver to take the engine any further; *Mallard* was run quietly on to Peterborough, and after a visit to Doncaster Works, where it was found that the engine needed no more attention than a renewal of the bearing metal in the middle big-end, she emerged once again, covered with glory, to take up her normal duties. *Mallard* now carries above the driving wheels two small commemorative plaques, encircled with laurel leaves, to commemorate her epic achievement.

So the speed "ceiling" had risen exactly in proportion to the gradual development of the Gresley design technique. On November 30th, 1934, "A1" Pacific No. 4472 *Flying Scotsman* had attained 100 m.p.h. for the first time, with 180 lb. steam pressure and the modifications to the valve-motion, resulting from the 1925 locomotive exchange, without which the attainment of the third figure probably would have been impossible. On March 5th, 1935, "A3" Pacific No. 2750 *Papyrus*, with 217 as compared with 207 tons of train, had lifted the maximum to 108 m.p.h.; this with 220 lb. steam pressure and a considerably larger superheater. Next came the exploits of the "A4" Pacifics Nos. 2509 *Silver Link* and 2512 *Silver Fox*, on September 27th, 1935, and August 27th, 1936, respectively, the former with 235 tons and the latter with 270 tons, in touching $112\frac{1}{2}$ and 113 m.p.h.; we had now come to the use of 250 lb. pressure, improved steam passages, 9-inch piston-valves, and complete external streamlining. Last of all, with twin blast-pipes and double chimney, on July 7th, 1938, the "A4" *Mallard* raised the maximum attainable speed to 126 m.p.h.—a figure at which it is likely to remain for a long time to come, if not, indeed, for all time, with any British steam locomotive of traditional design and layout.

9

Everyday Pacific Performance

To deal at all adequately with the performance of the Gresley Pacifics would need many pages of description. With the accelerations from 1932 onwards its quality went up by leaps and bounds, and it reached its zenith in the streamline years from 1935 to the outbreak of the Second World War. Even after the war began, notwithstanding the extent by which main line schedules were decelerated, for some time the curtailment of the principal services increased train loads on so enormous a scale that exceptional performances were still the rule, until the punishment of the engines made it absolutely necessary to restrain the loadings to more reasonable figures.

From 1935 onwards, although the streamline trains were head and shoulders in speed above all other services, many of the trains needed very hard locomotive work for timekeeping, especially in the Southern Area between King's Cross and Doncaster. Hardest of all was the "Flying Scotsman," with the new and extremely weighty set of stock introduced by Gresley in 1938, of which the fourteen coaches, all air-conditioned, had a tare weight of 504 tons. This had to be taken over the 105·5 miles from King's Cross to Grantham in 110 minutes start to stop, and on from there to York, 82·7 miles, in 83 minutes. Coming up, the York-Grantham stretch was allowed 86½ minutes, and then the Grantham-London run had to be made at an average of precisely a mile a minute, often in early summer and late autumn with a load of over 550 tons—one of the most exacting schedules in the whole country at that time.

Among other trains, the so-called "Breakfast Flyer" from Leeds was allowed only 100 minutes for the Grantham-King's Cross stretch, though a less weighty train. I was personally responsible for getting three other schedules pared to just within the 60 m.p.h. limit. They were those of the "Yorkshire Pullman" in each direction between King's Cross and Doncaster, which became 156 minutes down and 155 minutes up for the 156 miles, and the 50-minute schedule from Grantham to Doncaster, 50·5 miles, of the 5·45 p.m. from King's Cross. The then Superintendent of the Line, Western Area, Mr. V. M. Barrington-Ward, readily agreed to the small cuts in the timings of these trains that would add 362 miles to the L.N.E.R. mile-a-minute mileage, in view of the strong advertising point that the L.M.S.R. was making at that period of its similarly-timed runs.

The competence with which the Pacifics tackled these tasks was a perpetual delight to any recorder who, like myself, was travelling constantly up and down the East Coast main line during those halcyon years. Whether one found an "A1," an "A3" or an "A4" locomotive at the head of one's train made little difference; loss of time by locomotive was a rare event. Moreover, the advent of the streamliners seemed to have put all the staff "on their toes"; the track had been brought up to a superb condition; the signalling had been greatly improved and adapted to high speed standards; the operating authorities, from the top downwards, took the utmost pains to see that the line was kept clear for the faster trains, even through such bottle-necks as from Greenwood to Potter's Bar; and, above all, the engine-crews, whether in the streamline links or not, had caught the high speed infection, and the effect was stimulating to a degree.

It was nothing unusual, with a heavy down express of 450 to 500 tons weight, notwithstanding the long initial climb from the terminus out to Potter's Bar, to cover the 76·4 miles to Peterborough in 75 to 77 minutes. A common time for the lovely racing stretch of 27·0 miles from Hitchin to Huntingdon would be something between 21 and 22 minutes, and would include a top speed of between 85 and 90 m.p.h. past Three Counties. One typical record of mine shows "A3" No. 2505 *Cameronian*, on the down "Flying Scotsman," losing 4 minutes by a very bad signal check at Hitchin, and for all that passing Peterborough in 76 min. 19 sec.—$72\frac{1}{4}$ minutes net—with speeds of $83\frac{1}{2}$ m.p.h. beyond Sandy, $72\frac{1}{2}$ at St. Neot's, $77\frac{1}{2}$ at Offord, $64\frac{1}{2}$ at milepost 62, and $86\frac{1}{2}$ at Holme, this with a 460-ton train. Even with 540 tons No. 4475 *Flying Fox*, after a 20 m.p.h. permanent way slowing at Knebworth, took no

Flying Scotsman in 1949, now Class "A3" No. 60103, with banjo dome. The famous locomotive is near Potters Bar with the 10.15 a.m. Leeds and Harrogate—King's Cross express.

[*E. D. Bruton*]

PACIFICS
AT WORK

[C. R. L. Coles

ON THE EX-GREAT CENTRAL—Pacifics were first seen in regular service on the old Great Central main line in 1938, were withdrawn at the outbreak of war, and were reintroduced in 1949. "A3" No. 60048 Doncaster passes Sudbury with an up Cup Final Excursion from Leicester in 1949.

[E. R. Wethersett

ON FREIGHT—With over 200 Pacifics on the East Coast Route, it is quite common to see one on freight duty. "A3" No. 70 *Gladiateur*, on a down goods, makes a leisurely ascent of the lengthy climb from Berwick up to Burnmouth.

[C. C. B. Herbert

RUNNING IN—No. 4472 *Flying Scotsman* ambles along with a lightweight local train (one old triplet articulated set and two bogies) near Abbots Ripton.

(Above)
IN BLUE LIVERY with B.R. emblem on the tender, "A3" No. 60086 *Gainsborough* climbs away from Bramhope Tunnel, N.E.R., with the up "Queen of Scots."

(Left)
THE REAR VIEW of a Gresley Pacific is impressive. "A3" No. 41 *Salmon Trout* pulls out of Edinburgh Waveley.

[*H. Weston,*
C. C. B. Herbert

more than 77 min. 50 sec., or $75\frac{3}{4}$ minutes net. Mr. O. S. Nock has recorded a run with "A3" No. 2744 *Grand Parade* which is very likely a record exit from King's Cross with a load as heavy as 530 tons, for Peterborough was passed in an actual time of 73 min. 55 sec., with a maximum of $87\frac{1}{2}$ m.p.h. at Three Counties and an average of 77·8 m.p.h. over the Hitchin-Huntingdon stretch.

One of the most amazing performances ever put up, not by an "A3," but by an "A1," is set out in the last column of Table 3; it was timed by Mr. R. E. Charlewood. The train concerned was the down "Scarborough Flyer," allowed no more than the even three hours to run the 188·2 miles from King's Cross to York, and in mid-season a considerably weightier proposition than any of the streamliners, though, of course, on an easier timing by 23 minutes than the "Corona-tion." On this occasion Driver Duddington, the renowned Doncaster expert, was at the regulator of No. 4473 *Solario*, and received all the necessary stimulus to an exceptional effort after the train had had to make an emergency stop at Welwyn Garden City; the roof-board of a coach had come adrift and had been noticed by a watchful signalman. The express had been delayed 3 minutes on starting by an exceptional rush of passengers, and as a result of this and the stop was $10\frac{1}{2}$ minutes late through Hitchin.

Then *Solario* put up a meteoric performance. Allowing for the loss by a slight signal check at Yaxley, her driver succeeded in making the engine keep exactly the schedule time of the "Silver Jubilee"—with 395 as compared with 265 tons of train!—from Hitchin right through to Selby. By Doncaster the "Scarborough Flyer" had more than won back to schedule time, but Duddington still continued to blaze away, and in the end brought his train to a stand in York Station 5 minutes early, having completed the run in 172 min. 6 sec., or 162 minutes net, only 5 minutes more than the "Coronation's" 157-minute allowance. While the "A3," with such a load, could hardly be expected to maintain the streamline schedule up the hill from Peterborough to Stoke, her time of 38 min. 15 sec. for the 50·5 miles from Grantham to Doncaster probably was a record. It included such flighty proceedings at $81\frac{1}{2}$ m.p.h. round the Grantham curve and 75 over Retford level crossing!

TABLE 3.

Typical High Speed Runs with Gresley Pacifics

Engine No. / „ Name / Load, tons tare / „ „ full		§2509 Silver Link 220 235		§2509 Silver Link 254 270		§4491 Commonwealth of Australia 312 330		†4473 Solario 371 395	
Dist.		Times	Speeds	Times	Speeds	Times	Speeds	Times	Speeds
miles		min. sec.	m.p.h.	min. sec.	m.p.h.	min. sec.	m.p.h.	min. sec.	m.p.h.
0·0	KINGS CROSS	0 00	—	0 00	—	0 00	—	0 00	—
2·5	FINSBURY PARK	5 18	50	5 12	—	5 06	—	6 16	—
5·0	Wood Green	7 41	70½	7 44	61½	7 33	—	9 11	—
12·7	Potter's Bar	14 43	66	15 11	64	14 37	67	17 37	—
17·7	HATFIELD	18 22	90	19 09	*81	18 25	86½	21 55	77
								Sig. Stop	
23·5	Woolmer Green	22 42	76½	23 38	73	22 36	79	35 20	51½
28·6	Stevenage	26 49	80½/*68	27 45	77/73	26 28	90/*67	40 04	72
31·9	HITCHIN	29 23	—	30 21	80	28 56	88	42 38	80½
37·0	Arlesey	32 38	98/*86	33 54	90/86	32 15	94½	46 04	91
44·1	Sandy	37 17	92	38 53	82/88	37 03	90	51 02	85½
51·7	St. Neot's	42 19	88	44 21	80	42 15	83½	56 41	76
55·7	Offord	‡Sig Stop	—	47 39	*68	45 22	90/*70	59 51	81
58·9	HUNTINGDON	51 13	80½	50 00	76	47 40	80½	62 07	74
62·0	Milepost 62	53 35	80½	52 28	74	50 07	75	64 49	65½
69·4	Holme	58 36	98	57 39	93	55 07	98	70 30	83½
								Sigs	
75·0	Fletton Junction	62 19	90	61 53	71	59 08	—	75 21	*38
76·4	PETERBOROUGH	64 31	*21	63 46	*23½	61 20	*20	77 23	*26
79·5	Werrington Junction	68 08	74	67 39	75	65 16	—	81 27	60
84·8	Tallington	71 59	92	71 33	90	69 23	83½	86 18	—
88·6	Essendine	74 32	90	74 08	86½	72 04	85	89 36	68
92·2	Little Bytham	76 58	88	76 38	86	74 37	82	92 47	—
97·1	Corby Glen	80 30	80½/82	80 17	78/80	78 21	76½/78	97 30	60
100·1	Stoke	82 48	76½	82 39	75	80 48	68	100 27	57½
		p.w.s.							
105·5	GRANTHAM	87 25	*20	86 55	80/*63	85 17	75	104 40	81½
		—	—	—	—	p.w.s.	*25		
109·7	Barkstone	93 42	—	90 36	78	89 56	—	107 49	—
120·1	NEWARK	100 53	95½/*80	98 08	88/*82	97 08	90/*70	114 56	90/85
126·4	Carlton	105 50	*69/86½	103 16	*69/84	101 58	85	119 33	82
133·7	Markham	111 03	83½	108 46	75	107 16	76½	125 45	64
138·6	RETFORD	114 35	92/*65	112 33	83/*71	110 58	88/*67	129 40	84/*75
143·9	Ranskill	118 33	92/*70	116 37	87/*66	115 08	86½/*65	133 31	81½
149·5	Milepost 149½	122 47	74/83½	121 19	67/81	119 50	67	137 48	71/83½
156·0	DONCASTER	128 12	*72½	126 40	*67	125 11	*62	142 55	*67
160·2	Shaftholme Junction	131 23	83½	130 11	79/*69	128 42	eased	146 20	—
166·0	Balne	135 21	92	134 42	84	133 15	„	150 51	76
173·0	Brayton Junction	140 09	93½	139 47	87	138 40	„	156 11	—
174·4	SELBY	141 55	*30	141 18	*32	140 40	*28	157 53	*34
178·5	Riccall	146 07	75	145 49	72½	145 28	eased	162 31	62
184·0	Naburn	150 01	90	149 59	82½	150 01	„	167 14	72
186·2	Chaloner's Whin Jct.	152 00	*52	152 03	*53	152 13	„	169 08	—
188·2	YORK	†155 02	*20	†154 38	*27	155 36	„	172 06	—
188·2	¶Net times (min.)	¶148	—	¶155	—	154		162	—

* Speed restriction. † Passing time. ‡ At Paxton box, 53·7 miles, 44 min. 8 sec. to 45 min. 8 sec. from King's Cross. § Class "A4". † Class "A1." ¶ Equivalent time to dead stop.

There were a few occasions on which, owing to minor faults developing in "A4" Pacifics, "A3" engines have been commandeered at short notice to work the streamline trains. Two such substitutions took place in one week in March, 1939; and not only did No. 2595 *Trigo* and No. 2507 *Singapore*, in the capable hands of Driver Nash and Fireman Gilbey, prove themselves equal to the task, but on both days time lost by late starts was regained. *Trigo* covered the 268·3 miles from Newcastle to King's Cross in 229 minutes, or 225 minutes net; *Singapore* made the even more notable time of 227½ minutes, or 222½ minutes net, so doing the entire run at an average speed of 72·3 m.p.h. This is probably the fastest time that has ever been achieved by rail between Tyneside and London.

A journey on one of the streamline trains was always, of course, an experience of the greatest interest to the recorder of locomotive performance. In Table 3 I have set out the details of three such runs in the down direction, the speeds of which seem hardly believable in present-day schedule conditions. On the first, *Silver Link*, with the seven-coach load of 235 tons that was invariable until the eighth vehicle was built into the train, had made the usual energetic start, with speed rising to 90 m.p.h. at Hatfield and 98 at Arlesey, when we were brought to a dead stand for signals at Paxton, between St. Neot's and Offord. This was a most unusual occurrence, seeing that it was customary to keep two complete signal sections clear ahead of each of the streamliners. Here we stood for sixty seconds precisely.

Starting away again like a rocket, *Silver Link* attained 80 m.p.h. in no more than 5 miles and passed Huntingdon, 5·2 miles, in 6 min. 5 sec.; the 3 miles at 1 in 200 to milepost 62 were surmounted at a steady 80 and down the other side we touched 98 once again, so clearing Fletton Junction in 17 min. 11 sec. from the dead start at Paxton, 21·3 miles away! We were only a minute late through Peterborough—61 minutes net for the 76·4 miles from London—and despite a subsequent permanent way check, we passed Retford on time. At eleven different points on the journey speed rose to between 90 and 98 m.p.h.; and of these maxima the most notable were those attained on level track, such as 92 m.p.h. at Tallington, a recovery in 5 miles from 69 over Muskham troughs to 90 at

Crow Park, the steady 90-93½ over some miles between Shaftholme Junction and Selby, and the very unusual 90 before Naburn.

Finally, we reached Darlington, 232·3 miles from King's Cross, in 194 min. 40 sec., 3¼ minutes early; I calculate that the net times were 121 minutes to Doncaster, 147¾ minutes to passing York at a walking pace, and 187¼ minutes to Darlington—a net gain of 10¾ minutes on schedule. Over the 160·3 miles from Potter's Bar to Brayton Junction, Selby, our net average speed—allowing for the Paxton stop and Grantham permanent way check, but not for any of the regular speed restrictions—worked out at 81·4 m.p.h. throughout.

The second run in Table 3 is the one made, with Sparshatt at the regulator of *Silver Link*, on the test trip mentioned in Chapter 7, in which this run is described in full. On this occasion, in August, 1936, the dynamometer car had been added to the normal seven-coach formation of the "Silver Jubilee," bringing the total weight up to 270 tons.

The third run in this table was the inaugural down run of the "Coronation," already mentioned in Chapter 8, with Driver Dron in charge of No. 4491 *Commonwealth of Australia*. Perhaps the most brilliant feature of this run was the starting time of 18 min. 25 sec. from King's Cross to Hatfield, with a 330-ton load; all the way we were doing well, and the time of 125 min. 11 sec. past Doncaster, 3¼ minutes less than schedule, then justified the driver in easing his engine perceptibly. But even so, York was reached in 155 min. 36 sec., 1½ minutes early. There is no need to give details of the continuation of these runs north of York, for in those days, as already mentioned, the demands of the timetable were much less exacting over the North Eastern and Scottish Areas than over the Southern Area, so that by York, going north, the hardest of the work was over.

When the three-aspect signalling came into use between York and Northallerton, however, there was some slight adjustment of schedules, and matters north of York brightened up considerably. I had one northbound run with No. 2512 *Silver Fox*, and the eight-car "Silver Jubilee," 265 tons in gross weight, on which we reached 94 m.p.h. on dead level track, and covered 15·4 miles of level or slightly rising track at an average speed of 90·6 m.p.h. Since the war, on a test run made in 1946, the same engine, travelling south with a 207-ton train, and with Driver Leonard of York in charge, ran the level 27·0 miles from Northallerton to Skelton Bridge in 17 min. 58 sec., at an average of almost exactly 90 m.p.h. for the whole distance, touching a top speed of 93½ m.p.h. at Raskelf; cut-off was 35 per cent. throughout, with regulator wide open.

If such speeds could be attained and maintained by Gresley's "A4s" on level track, it is a matter of no surprise that maxima of over 100 m.p.h. could be reached with the utmost ease downhill. I have referred previously to the fact that *Silver Link*, on her immortal "Silver Jubilee" trial trip, was keeping up a steady 109 m.p.h. after the descent from Stevenage had flattened out to level at Tempsford, and even went over the "hump" at St. Neot's, with approach grades of 1 in 330 up, at 104½ m.p.h. Mr. O. S. Nock has recorded a run with *Commonwealth of Australia*, with 325 tons on the up "Coronation," on which a maximum of 105 m.p.h., attained at Essendine, was continued, with fluctuations between 105 and 106, for 6¾ miles during which the gradient flattens gradually from 1 in 200 to level. In all her locomotive history, Britain has never possessed speedier engines than these.

To show the work of which the same engines are capable with really heavy loads, in Table 4 I have set out the details of two runs from Grantham to King's Cross, both with trains of 500 tons weight or over. On the first of these "A4" Pacific No. 4466 *Herring Gull* was faced with the task of working the 510-ton "Flying Scotsman" over the 105·5 miles to King's Cross in 105½ minutes, and did so comfortably, with 3 minutes to spare. While the sustained 90 m.p.h. from Little Bytham to Essendine with this load is a matter for remark, something considerably more notable is the time of 22 min. 21 sec. for the 27·0 miles from Huntingdon to Hitchin, against the rising tendency of the road—a very fast time for the down direction but an amazing time for an up train so loaded.

Yet the same feat was very nearly repeated by *Osprey* with her 500-ton load, as shown in the next column. The latter train was the 5.30 p.m. from Leeds to King's Cross, and we

TABLE 4.

Typical Heavy Load Runs with Gresley "A4" Pacifics

Engine No. ,, Name Load, tons tare ,, ,, full	4466 Herring Gull 478 510		† 4494 †Osprey 474 500	
Dist.		Times	Speeds	Dist.	Times	Speeds
miles		min. sec.	m.p.h.	miles	min. sec.	m.p.h.
0·0	GRANTHAM	0 00	—	0·0	0 00	—
5·4	Stoke	10 02	40	5·4	9 16	46
8·4	Corby Glen	13 00	—	8·4	12 11	74
13·3	Little Bytham	17 23	90	13·3	16 05	—
16·9	Essendine	19 49	90	16·9	18 56	77½
20·7	Tallington	22 25	—	20·7	22 03	—
26·0	Werrington Junction	26 35	*60	26·0	26 52	*60
				29·1	30 50	—
29·1	PETERBOROUGH	30 23	*25	0·0	0 00	—
30·5	Fletton Junction	33 00	—	1·4	3 45	—
36·1	Holme	38 52	71½	7·0	9 25	71¼
42·0	Abbot's Ripton	44 25	53½	12·9	14 39	57
46·6	HUNTINGDON	48 49	76½	17·5	18 54	76½
49·5	Offord	51 09	72½	20·4	21 17	71⅛
53·8	St. Neot's	54 45	68	24·7	25 03	64½
58·0	Tempsford	58 12	77½	28·9	28 38	75
61·4	Sandy	60 50	76½	32·3	31 23	77½
64·4	Biggleswade	63 14	69	35·3	33 47	70⅜
68·5	Arlesey	66 41	74	39·4	37 13	75
73·6	HITCHIN	71 10	60	44·5	41 38	64⅛
76·9	Stevenage	74 52	51	47·8	44 59	58½
80·5	Knebworth	78 34	—	51·4	48 19	—
83·5	Welwyn North	81 28	—	54·4	50 58	—
87·8	HATFIELD	84 53	79	58·7	54 26	79
92·8	Potter's Bar	89 10	66	63·7	59 09	58½
96·3	New Barnet	92 14	75	67·2	62 28	eased
100·5	Wood Green	95 47	*64	71·4	66 02	—
103·0	FINSBURY PARK	98 17	—	73·9	69 03	—
105·5	KING'S CROSS	102 39	—	76·4	73 44	—

* Speed restriction.   † No. 4500 Sir Ronald Matthews Grantham to Peterborough.

had been delayed at Doncaster, in marshalling the load, by the obstinate refusal of two buckeye couplers to disengage, notwithstanding the combined six-cylinder effort of a "K3" Mogul and an "A4" Pacific to make them do so. Eventually we got away from Doncaster 18 minutes late, behind "A4" 4-6-2 No. 4500 Sir Ronald Matthews. Time recovery began at once. To Grantham we ran the 50·5 miles in 52 min. 12 sec., picking up 4¾ minutes, and that notwithstanding a permanent way slowing at Tuxford. From Grantham we ran the 29·1 miles to Peterborough, even though not exceeding 77½ m.p.h. "down the hill," in 30 min. 50 sec., and another 3¼ minutes of the arrears were wiped off.

But it was Driver Ovenden, on No. 4494 *Osprey*, which was substituted for *Sir Ronald Matthews* at Peterborough, who made the pace. For he gained no less than 11¼ minutes from Peterborough to King's Cross, and so arrived dead on time (we had overstayed our allowance at Peterborough by a minute). On this run outstanding work uphill was added to that on the level, particularly the minimum speed of 58½ m.p.h. at Stevenage after the whole of the long climb from the Ouse valley, finishing with miles at 1 in 200. So well had we done, that Ovenden was able to ease his engine after Hatfield for quite a moderate run into the terminus; had we repeated the last sprint of *Herring Gull* we might have completed the 76·4 miles from Peterborough to King's Cross in just over 72 minutes, which would have been a gain on schedule of 13 minutes from Peterborough alone.

It was during the first year or two of the war that the Gresley Pacifics had to handle their biggest trains, many of which were heavier than anything ever hauled before or since by unassisted locomotives on passenger service in Great Britain. Twenty-coach loads were common on trains like the "Flying Scotsman," and it was nothing unusual, particularly in the up direction, for 21, 22, or even 23 to be taken, crammed with passengers from end to end. At the time I published details of a run with this train, timed by the Rev. G. C. Stead, in which "A4" Pacific No. 4901, then named *Capercaillie*, hauling a 22-coach load of 665 tons tare and not less than 730 tons gross, ran the 25·0 miles between Otterington and Poppleton Junction, again on the high speed Darlington-York stretch, in 19 min. 57 sec., at an average of no less than 75·9 m.p.h., reaching a top speed of 78½ m.p.h. on the level at Raskelf. It has been calculated that the drawbar horse-power needed for such a feat would be in the region of 2,200 continuously.

By contrast with her flying exploits on the "Silver Jubilee," on April 5th, 1940, *Silver Link* was faced with the herculean task of lifting a 25-coach train out of King's Cross—so lengthy, in fact, that the head of the train, engine included, was in Gasworks Tunnel, and a man had to be sent to the tunnel mouth to give the driver the "right away." A full 16 minutes elapsed before this vast assemblage of 750 tons tare and 830 to

850 tons gross, made its appearance at Finsbury Park, but from there the overtaxed "A4" succeeded in running the 103·0 miles to Grantham in 123 minutes. To Grantham *Silver Link* had dropped 11 minutes, but from Grantham, with 105 minutes allowed to York, 52 minutes on to Darlington, and 50 minutes from Darlington to Newcastle, the additional loss was 4 minutes only.

It may be added that even one of the original "A1" engines, designed by Gresley for the haulage of 600-ton trains, No. 2549 *Persimmon*, at about the same period worked a 24-coach train of 759 tons tare and some 850 tons gross from Peterborough to King's Cross in 96 minutes, losing 2 minutes only on the 94-minute schedule then in force for the Leeds train concerned. During those war years the London & North Eastern Railway management had good cause to be grateful to Sir Nigel Gresley for his "big engine" policy, which had provided them with a stud of locomotives of such exceptional power and reliability to meet the tremendous strain of war conditions.

A belated but emphatic tribute to the success of Gresley's "A4" Pacific design came with the extensive locomotive exchange trials of 1948, when engines of this type worked between King's Cross and Leeds, Euston and Carlisle, Paddington and Plymouth, and Waterloo and Exeter, in competition with London Midland Region "Duchess" Pacifics and rebuilt "Royal Scot" 4-6-0s, Western Region "King" 4-6-0s, and Southern Region "Merchant Navy" Pacifics. The engines used were *Mallard, Seagull* and *Lord Faringdon.* Unfortunately that susceptible middle big-end gave trouble on three different "foreign" runs, either in the preliminary or the actual test weeks, necessitating the removal of *Mallard* and *Seagull* from their trains, which was a blot on an otherwise splendid record.

The finest feats were those of *Seagull*, coming up from Plymouth on May 5th. Permanent way relaying brought Driver Burgess down to 16 m.p.h. in Plympton Station, right at the foot of the formidable 1 in 41 climb to Hemerdon box. Yet, with cut-off opened out to 50 per cent. and regulator wide open, the engine spurted to 24 m.p.h. and then gamely lifted her 350-ton train up the terrific incline without the veriest suspicion of a slip, and without the speed at any point falling below 18½ m.p.h.—a magnificent performance. Later in the same journey, and now with 525 tons, *Seagull* streaked out of Taunton to such purpose that we ran 25·4 miles from the start to Alford, largely with grades against the engine, in 25 min. 10 sec.—a feat that I have never equalled with a comparably loaded Great Western engine. Moreover, the Official Report reveals that the "A4" supremacy extended also to coal and water consumption. Through the entire series of exchange tests, the average "A4" coal consumption, 3·06 lb. per drawbar-horsepower-hour, and water consumption, 24·32 lb. per drawbar-horsepower-hour, were the lowest of all the engines tested, whether express passenger, mixed traffic or freight. The nearest approach in coal consumption was the L.M.R. " Duchess " 4-6-2, with an average of 3·12 lb. The standard Western Region " King," tested only on the Western and Eastern Regions, when using Yorkshire coal, to which its blast and draught arrangements were unsuited, burned 3·57 lb. of coal and evaporated 28·58 lb. of water per drawbar-horsepower-hour. Even when, in later months, a standard "King" was tested with Welsh coal between Paddington and Plymouth only, with all the advantages of running over its own main line, the consumption remained at 3·33 lb. per drawbar-horsepower-hour, and a "King" experimentally fitted with high temperature superheat, and also burning Welsh coal, could not bring the figure below 3·10 lb. By comparison, when the "A4" with Yorkshire coal had the advantage of working over E.R. metals only, the coal consumption was as low as 2·92 lb. per drawbar-horsepower-hour.

So, in the 1948 exchange, Gresley succeeded with a vengeance, even if posthumously, in reversing the results of the historic exchange of 1925! As I have already mentioned, full deatils of what happened in both these exchange trials are given in my recent book, "The Locomotive Exchanges, 1870-1948," so that there is no need to devote further attention to the subject.

10

Numbers, Names and Notes

In this chapter it is necessary to summarise a part of the information which has gone before, and to add certain items of interest, before our survey of the Gresley Pacifics can be regarded as complete. First of all, as to numbers and names. Appendix I gives the numbers and names of the whole of the 114 6 ft. 8 in. Pacifics built during the Gresley *regime*, between 1922 and 1938 inclusive, in the order in which the engines were built. In parallel columns there are shown the original L.N.E.R. numbers, the L.N.E.R. numbers under the Thompson renumbering scheme of 1946, and the present British Railways numbers.

The names of the series, in the course of time, have become rather a mixed bag. After starting away with *Great Northern*, *Sir Frederick Banbury* (one of the G.N.R. directors up to the time of the grouping) and *Flying Scotsman*, Gresley began the long list of names of racehorses which at various times had won the country's classic events; of these he used 74 in all, interrupted by *Prince of Wales* (No. 2553), *Centenary* (No. 2555), which was named to commemorate the Railway Centenary of 1925, and *William Whitelaw* (No. 2563), named after the Chairman of the newly-formed London & North Eastern Railway. After the "A4" class had been introduced, the gentleman last named was promoted to "A4" rank, and No. 4462 *Great Snipe* was changed from winged to merely pedestrian status by being renamed *William Whitelaw*, while the previous two-legged *William Whitelaw* (No. 2563) became the four-legged *Tagalie*. The racehorse *motif* had some odd results at times, as, for example, when the astonished delegates to a Methodist Conference found *Robert the Devil* at the head of their special train, whether by accident or design is not related.

The racehorse names continued throughout the "A3" series of Pacifics, but with the introduction of the "A4s" a change took place. The first four of these, Nos. 2509 to 2512 inclusive, received names appropriate to the "Silver Jubilee" theme—*Silver Link*, *Quicksilver*, *Silver King* and *Silver Fox*. When "A4" building recommenced with No. 4482, the first bird names were introduced, and would have continued without interruption but for decisions taken when the "Coronation" and "West Riding Limited" streamliners were introduced. Special names thus were conferred on Nos. 4488 to 4492 inclusive and 4495 and 4496 for the working of these trains. But No. 4488 originally was named *Osprey* before becoming *Union of South Africa*; while for No. 4489 the first nameplates made, but never used, were *Buzzard*, then the engine emerged and ran as *Woodcock*, and this was changed within a matter of months to *Dominion of Canada*. The *Woodcock* nameplates were transferred to No. 4493 and the *Osprey* nameplates to No. 4494. Nos. 4495 and 4496 were named *Golden Fleece* (after a week or so as *Great Snipe*), and *Golden Shuttle* respectively, and another exception to the bird series was No. 4498 *Sir Nigel Gresley*, named after the designer.

After the Second World War there arose a sudden passion to immortalise directors and officers of the pre-nationalisation railways by naming engines after them, and, as a result, many of the beautiful bird names disappeared. Those lost in this way are *Kestrel*, *Sea Eagle*, *Osprey*, *Great Snipe* and *Herring Gull* (mentioned in an earlier chapter), *Gadwall*, *Pochard*, *Garganey*, *Capercaillie* and *Peregrine*. With the most profound respect to the distinguished gentlemen concerned, one cannot help wondering if the name *Andrew K. McCosh* can have quite the same publicity appeal as *Osprey*, or if *Walter K. Whigham* is any adequate substitute for *Sea Eagle* or *Miles Beevor* for *Kestrel*, to name but three typical examples.

Recent events may cause *Empire of India* (No. 4490) to be changed to *Dominion of India*. To mark his great services to the Allied cause in the recent war, General Eisenhower was honoured in the naming after him of No. 4496, previously *Golden Shuttle* and now *Dwight D. Eisenhower*. It may be added that originally Nos. 4466 and 4467 were to have been *Hirondelle* and *Condor*; but eventually *Herring Gull* and *Wild Swan* were the names chosen. *Mallard*, typical genus of wild duck, proved a worthy successor indeed to the *Wild Duck* of historic exploits on the L.N.W.R. years earlier. One curious example of changed names concerns an "A1," No. 2564, which ran at first as *Knight of the Thistle*; but apparently there was some technical error in this designation, which was amended later to *Knight of Thistle*. In Appendix I the earlier names of engines which had their names altered subsequently are shown in brackets, with the present names following.

Throughout the "A1" and "A3" series, Gresley applied his engine names in curved cast brass nameplates fitted above the driving wheel splashers. With the advent of the "A4" engines, splashers disappeared, and something new had to be devised. Straight nameplates for the smokebox sides, similar to those used already on the "P2" 2-8-2 engines, were cast for *Silver Link*, and duly applied, but their appearance did not meet with the approval of Gresley's daughter, who acted as his "art adviser," and they were removed. He was then content with the singularly poor substitute of painting the names, not even in Gill Sans lettering, along the middle of the streamlined casing. When No. 4482 *Golden Eagle* was turned out of Doncaster, however, the elegant straight nameplates, fixed on the smokebox sides, reappeared, and have since become standard, the "Silver Jubilee" engines being altered to correspond when their colour was changed from grey to blue. The seven "Coronation" and "West Riding" engines, with No. 4498 *Sir Nigel Gresley*, were distinguished by receiving chromium-plated nameplates, railway initials, numbers and certain other decorations, the initials and numbers in relief, and this practice also later became standardised for engines of this class. With the renumbering in the 60,000s, however, the relief lettering has disappeared.

Hitherto I have referred to the Gresley Pacifics only by their original L.N.E.R. numbers, which, as previously mentioned, were bestowed in somewhat haphazard fashion, as blocks of numbers became available at the time of construction. The various sequences, in order of construction, were 4470 to 4481 (previously G.N.R. Nos. 1470 to 1481), 2543 to 2582, 2743 to 2752, 2595 to 2599, 2795 to 2797, 2500 to 2512, 4482 to 4498, 4462 to 4469, 4499 and 4500, and 4900 to 4903. Eventually therefore, there was one unbroken series from 2543 to 2582, another from 4462 to 4500, with Nos. 2500 to 2512, 2595 to 2599, 2743 to 2752, 2795 to 2797, and 4900 to 4903.

During the Thompson *regime* a complete renumbering of the whole of the London & North Eastern Railway locomotive stock eventually was decided on. It had an interim phase, during which a few of the Gresley Pacifics received numbers in the 500s and 600s. Then came the final L.N.E.R. numbering, with the "A4s" numbered consecutively from 1 to 34, and the "A3s" from 35 to 112. This renumbering began in 1946, and two years later, the L.N.E.R. having now become a part of British Railways, the work had to begin all over again with 60,000 added to the L.N.E.R. numbers. A certain proportion of the Thompson renumbering was done in the same sequence as that in which the engines were built, but not all. In particular, the "A4" Pacific serial numbering to-day is nothing like the building sequence, for the "personalities" among the engine names were almost all moved up to the "top of the form," to take the numbers 1 to 8 (except *Miles Beevor*, *Walter K. Whigham*, and *Lord Faringdon*, who were not commemorated in this way until after the renumbering had taken place, and so got left among the birds), and were followed by the "Dominions" and the "Silver Jubilee" series before the bird names began. This has involved a considerable rearrangement.

A word may now be said about Pacific colours. London & North Eastern green and standard lining was carried on uninterruptedly until the appearance of *Silver Link* and her three sisters in 1935, painted in silver-grey with the side valances in a darker grey shade and the sloping smokebox front and back. At first *Silver Link* had her light grey sides carried right into the sharp angle made by the sloping front and valance at their convergence above the buffer-beam, but later this corner was cut off by carrying the black of the smokebox round the sides in a graceful curve, considerably improving the side view of the engine. This became the standard method for the remaining "Silver Jubilee" engines.

As "A4" building recommenced, with No. 4482, the new "A4s" at first were painted and lined in standard green.

When the "Coronation" was about to be introduced, however, a series of experiments was tried with various shades of blue, all on No. 4488, until finally the attractive shade of Garter blue was decided on. During these experiments No. 4489 was running in workshop grey. With the blue there was combined a dark red finish for the wheels, the whole making for a most striking appearance. Later the "Silver Jubilee" Pacifics and all the green "A4s" were repainted in blue, and the entire class became uniform in appearance. After the depressing black interlude of the Second World War, Garter blue was reinstated.

An experiment was tried by Thompson when he rebuilt No. 4470 with a dark Royal blue shade, similar to that of the old Great Eastern Railway. In the new British Railways painting scheme, all the Gresley Pacifics, both "A3" and "A4", qualify for the new standard blue livery.

The Gresley Pacifics have had their share of serious casualties. Of these by far the worst, apart from the destruction by bombing of No. 4469, was the accident in which No. 2744 *Grand Parade* was involved at Castlecary, between Edinburgh and Glasgow, on December 10th, 1937. In a thick snowstorm the Pacific was working the 4.3 p.m. Edinburgh—Glasgow express when the driver overran signals at danger, and at a full 60 m.p.h. ran into the rear of the 2 p.m. from Dundee to Glasgow, which was held up at Castlecary by a signal failure, 35 passengers being killed. The rear end of the latter train was smashed up beyond recognition, and the leading vehicles of the Edinburgh express were badly damaged, which is not surprising in view of the calculation that the collision absorbed some 54,000 ft.-tons of energy. The damage to *Grand Parade* herself was so extreme that the No. 2744 which emerged from Doncaster subsequently, and now carries the number 60090, was practically a new engine.

In most of the other serious main line accidents of later years on the L.N.E.R., whether collisions or derailments, the engines have been "V2" 2-6-2s and not Pacifics. Of unusual casualties to Gresley Pacifics one was on May 10th, 1926, when No. 2565 *Merry Hampton* was deliberately derailed by strikers at Cramlington, Northumberland, during the coal dispute of that year, when hauling the up "Flying Scotsman", though fortunately at so slow a speed that relatively little damage was done. A far more serious derailment was that of October 26th, 1947, in which *Merry Hampton*, strange to relate, was involved once again. The engine was working the southbound Sunday "Scotsman," and the driver, carrying on the footplate an unauthorised "passenger," ran past all warning signals of engineering work in progress south of Goswick, in Northumberland, and had eleven of his fifteen coaches off the road on the reverse curve leading into the up relief line, to which his train was being diverted; 28 lives were lost.

One extraordinary accident in which an "A4" was concerned, though the engine itself suffered no damage whatsoever, occurred on the evening of Sunday, February 4th, 1945, when the 6 p.m. express was leaving King's Cross for Leeds and Bradford. The load was 17 coaches of about 590 tons weight, and the engine, No. 2512 *Silver Fox*, stalled in Gasworks Tunnel. Eventually the train got on the move, but when the driver thought he was moving forwards, actually the train was moving backwards. The road had been re-set after the train had entered the tunnel, but when the King's Cross signalman saw the tail of the train reappearing, he tried hastily to reverse the switch, to get the train back into the platform it had just left. He was a second or two too late. As a result, the points moved between the two bogies of the rear coach, and several coaches were derailed, skewing themselves across the track and demolishing a signal bridge; two passengers were killed.

As to special characteristics of individual Gresley Pacifics previous chapters have said almost all that is necessary, and the notes in Appendix I summarise the information. One curious experiment may be mentioned, however, Although these engines have never suffered to any extent from drifting exhaust, an experiment was tried with "A3" Pacific No. 2747 *Coronach* in which the upper part of the smokebox front was cut away to form an opening, curved on top concentrically with the smokebox, and straight below, where the opening finished well above the smokebox door handles. Inside, an inclined partition shut off the interior of the smokebox, and where the partition reached the top of the smokebox, an opening was made in the latter, at the back of the chimney. The idea of the two openings and the inclined plane between them was to make an up-draught, when the engine was running at speed, which would catch the exhaust from the chimney and lift it well above the cab. A variety of similar experiments was tried on No. 2751 *Humorist*, both before and after that engine had been fitted with double exhaust and a double chimney.

[E. Treacy]

DOUBLE-CHIMNEY "A4"—No. 4901 *Capercaillie* (now *Sir Charles Newton*) emerges from Potters Bar Tunnel with a down King's Cross—Newcastle express.

(Above)

THE NEW NON-STOP—"A4" No. 60033 *Seagull* approaches Welwyn Garden City with the up "Capitals Limited."

[*F. R. Hebron*

(Left)

BADGE presented to "A4" No. 27 *Merlin* by the R.N. Shore Establishment, H.M.S. *Merlin;* now fixed to the side of the boiler.

[*C. C. B. Herbert*

(Right upper)

WORLD'S RECORD HOLDER—"A4" No. 22 *Mallard*, showing on the side of the boiler one of the plaques commemorating her 126 m.p.h. record.

[*British Railways*

(Right Lower)

LIGHT DUTIES—"A4s," too, can be seen on local and freight duties to-day. No. 60021 *Wild Swan* passes Eaton Wood with an up stopping train.

[*M. P. Dove*

[F. R. Hebron

IN NEW B.R. BLUE LIVERY—"A4" No. 60029 Woodcock roars through Hadley Wood Station with the down "Yorkshire Pullman."

11

The Gresley Conjugated Motion

Last of all, a word is needed concerning the controversy which has always raged, and doubtless will continue to do so, over the merits or demerits of the Gresley conjugated valve-motion. Its opponents would be hard put to it to dispute that many of the most notable feats of British express loco-motive performance, including the highest speed with steam on record, have been achieved by engines so fitted. Conversely, on their side of the argument, there is the fact of the heating troubles experienced with the middle big-ends of Gresley Pacifics, some on occasions which have brought these failures very prominently under notice, particularly those of *Silver Fox* and *Mallard* after the high speed tests of 1936 and 1938, and of *Mallard* and *Seagull* in the 1948 locomotive exchanges. Even the observer without technical knowledge will not fail to notice that the exhaust beats of a Gresley Pacific often are not in perfectly regular sequence, but that the engines tend to have a slightly syncopated beat which is acoustically obvious when they are working hard.

There are two reasons why the centre valve of an engine fitted with the Gresley derived motion tends to over-run. The first is the deflection of the stay supporting the main fulcrum of the 2 to 1 lever which takes its movement from the two outside valve-motions (and possibly some slight deflection of the lever itself), and the second is wear and tear of the pin joints of the conjugated gear. As compared with the original "K3" engines, Nos. 1000 to 1009, on which the over-running of the centre valve first became apparent, Gresley in his Pacifics had strengthened the stay referred to, and also had provided the fulcrums of both the main 2 to 1 levers and the "equal" levers of the gear with ball and roller bearings, to minimise wear; but even these modifications did not provide a complete cure. It has been estimated that by over-running the cut-off in the middle cylinder at high speeds may be 10 per cent. higher than that in the two outside cylinders.

It has never been possible to indicate an "A4" Pacific, because with the streamlined casing there is no footplating on which to mount the indicator and the observer. In his paper to the Institution of Locomotive Engineers, to which reference has been made previously, however, Mr. B. Spencer mentioned the indicating of "A3" Pacific No. 2751, *Humorist*, in which a comparison was made of the work done in the engine's three cylinders. At speeds up to 45 m.p.h. there was little difference; but from then on the over-running began to be perceptible. With a 540-ton train, at 57 m.p.h. the horsepowers developed by the two outside cylinders were 460 and 518 and by the middle cylinder 558; at 63 m.p.h. 394 and 472 outside and 547 inside; and at 75 m.p.h. 402 and 480 outside and as much as 585 inside. If there were such a difference at 75 m.p.h., to what point might the difference increase at 90 or 100 m.p.h.?

In the early days of the "A4" design, L.N.E.R. locomotive maintenance in general was of so high a standard that the derived motions could be kept in first-class running order, and so gave little trouble unless some particularly extravagant demand was made on the engines. Mention has been made already of some exceptional endurance feats, over considerable distances, of "A4" Pacifics on difficult assignments like the "Coronation" streamliner and the non-stop "Flying Scotsman," and these prove that the Gresley derived motion can stand up to any amount of hard work if properly maintained. But as the engines were turned into more general service, on a common-user basis, in the strenuous speed conditions of the years immediately before the Second World War, the middle big-end trouble began to increase to such an extent that something had to be done about it. Of all the Pacifics the "A4s" were always the most susceptible, for the streamlining reduces the amount of cool air circulating between the frames: moreover, it may make it difficult for a driver to detect an overheated bearing by his sense of smell until the trouble has reached serious proportions.

The first step taken was before the war, and it was one of prevention rather than cure. Through the middle crank-pin of each Pacific, "A1," "A3," and "A4" alike, a hole was drilled large enough to accommodate what is known colloquially as a "stink bomb," or, in more dignified parlance, a detector. This is a metal cylinder containing amyl acetate vapour, and closed at one end by a glass bulb and sprinkler of the type used in automatic fire extinguishers. At a predetermined temperature (about 160 deg. F.) this bulb bursts, and unlooses a smell of so pungent a description that it is almost certain to be noticed in the cab. Already these detectors have proved most valuable, making it possible to detect big-end heating even before the melting of the bearing metal, let alone the damage to or complete disintegration of the brasses which may follow a bad case of heating.

During the war things went from bad to worse. In the early days of the war the Pacifics were flogged unmercifully in handling trains of 700 to 800 tons gross weight, and sometimes even more, and with shortage of staff and materials the standard of maintenance fell steadily at the same time. For example, the grease lubrication of the 2-to-1 motion, until then invariably carried out by a fitter rather than the driver, went by default, as did various other kinds of skilled attention to their motion that the engines had been accustomed to receive. Wear in all the pins increased as a result of inadequate lubrication and of the failure to keep the derived gear clear of ash during smokebox cleaning; excessive mileage between overhauls took its toll; the quality of lubricating oil declined steadily. Thus the number of middle big-end failures went up by leaps and bounds.

Since the war there has been a substantial measure of recovery and at certain sheds in particular, in response to more careful attention and the allocation of individual engines to individual pairs of crews as far as possible, the Pacifics once again are beginning to show their characteristic reliability and prowess in performance. At the ripe age of 26 years, for example, in 1949 "A3" Pacific No. 60106 *Flying Fox*, stationed at Grantham, ran 8,689 miles on express trains in the four weeks between mid-May and mid-June; "A4" Pacific No. 60030 *Golden Fleece*, also from Grantham shed, completed 19,030 miles, mostly on the heavy "Flying Scotsman" and "Aberdonian" turns, between February 14th and May 3rd; while No. 60003 *Andrew K. McCosh* (of King's Cross shed) ran 4,528 miles in no more than 12 consecutive days. Nevertheless the three middle big-end failures which occurred during the 1948 locomotive exchanges with "A4" Pacifics which had been specially tuned up for the tests were abnormally high in relation to the mileage run, and brought this feature of the Gresley design into exceptional prominence.

What has just been written, therefore, will help to explain some of the developments which have taken place since Sir Nigel Gresley's untimely death in 1941. As an experiment, four of the "A4s", Nos. 60003, 60012, 60014 and 60031, have had their middle cylinders lined up to 17 in. diameter, $1\frac{1}{2}$ in. less than that of the outside cylinders. But while this may help to equalise the cylinder horsepowers at high speeds, it results in a very unequal effort from the three cylinders at lower speeds, as well as cutting down the tractive effort. In addition, all the Pacifics built by Gresley's successors have been provided with three independent sets of Walschaerts motion, one for each cylinder. The first experiments in this direction were made by Mr. E. Thompson in rebuilding the Gresley "P2" class 2-8-2 locomotives as Pacifics, and all subsequent new Pacific construction followed this lead. Certain of the Gresley Pacifics also have had their maximum cut-off increased from 65 to 75 per cent., though this change does not appear to be related to any of the modifications just mentioned.

The next step was to take the first engine of the entire Pacific series, No. 4470 *Great Northern* (now No. 60113), and so radically to transform it that the original designer would have some considerable difficulty in recognising his own handiwork, were he still living. To obtain room for the inside motion, the inside cylinders were moved forwards to drive on the leading coupled axle—a change which, by dividing the drive, violated one of Gresley's most cherished principles of design. To equalise connecting-rod lengths the outside cylinders, still driving on the middle coupled axle, were pushed backwards, the whole effect, externally, being very ungainly. The footplating was raised high from the buffer-beam to the cylinders, and higher still over the driving wheels, the whole of whose 6 ft. 8 in. diameter thus was uncovered; at first this height was continued right back to the cab, the side sheets of which were perched above it, but the effect was so hideous that eventually the Gresley cab-sides were restored. Above a smokebox of enormous length a double stovepipe chimney of repellent aspect was mounted: and smoke deflectors of an odd shape were added, with the nameplates *Great Northern* spread right across their width.

If this experiment had to be made, one can only regret that, of all the engines on which it might have been conducted, the original *Great Northern*, with all the stirring memories that she evokes of Gresley's designing genius, should have been the one chosen for such disfiguring attentions. This regret is only tempered by the fact that, owing to the extensive use of "pooled" parts in locomotive reconditioning work at Doncaster, very little of the original G.N.R. No. 1470 may have remained in the L.N.E.R. No. 4470 at the time of conversion.

The rebuilding of this engine, at first classified as "A1" but now as "A1/1," was intended as a model for later 6-ft. 8-in. Pacific construction, but when the first Peppercorn engines of the present "A1" series made their appearance, beginning with No. 60114, it was seen that there are considerable differences between the two. In particular, the bogie has been moved back, by no less than 2 ft. 5 in., to its original position, with the smokebox more or less central above it, though the ugly chimney, now pushed forward to the extreme front of the smokebox, still remains. Divided drive, with three separate sets of valve-motion, is continued, and permits the use of piston-valves of as large diameter as 10 in., which is certainly an advantage. One other important change in the Peppercorn engines is an increase in the firegrate area from the Gresley $41\frac{1}{4}$ sq. ft. to 50 sq. ft.

In these austere and strictly utilitarian days, the graceful locomotive lines initiated by Gresley are rapidly disappearing, and this, strangely enough, at a time when other countries, the United States in particular, are alive as never before to the publicity value of locomotive outline, colour and cleanliness. Would that such considerations had more weight here!

THE GRESLEY PACIFICS OF THE L.N.E.R.

Sir Nigel Gresley died on April 5th, 1941, in harness, as he himself surely would have wished. He had been Locomotive Engineer of the Great Northern Railway from 1911 to 1922, and Chief Mechanical Engineer of the London & North Eastern Railway from the formation of the latter company in 1923 until his death, a total of thirty years. Many honours came to him during his career, including the O.B.E. for his services in the First World War, awarded in 1920, the honorary degree of Doctor of Science from Manchester University in 1936, and the dignity of Knight Bachelor in the Birthday Honours of the same year.

In no uncertain fashion has he left the impress of his personality on the locomotive practice of Great Britain. Fortunately many of his designs, and his Pacifics in particular, can still hold their own with their later competitors, and are likely to remain with us for a long time in the form in which he built them, as a reminder both of one of the most exciting periods in British locomotive history and also of one of the most able and versatile of all British locomotive engineers. We salute his honoured memory.

Appendix I

THE GRESLEY PACIFICS—NUMBERS, NAMES AND CLASSES

For Key to Notes, see page 122.

L.N.E.R. Original No.	Thompson Renumbering	British Railways No.	Name*	Original Class	Date of Building	Present Class	Notes
4470	113	60113	Great Northern	A1	1922	A1/1	A
4471	102	60102	Sir Frederick Banbury	A1	,,	A3	B
4472	103§	60103	Flying Scotsman	,,	1923	,,	CP
4473	104	60104	Solario	,,	,,	,,	—
4474	105	60105	Victor Wild	,,	,,	,,	D
4475	106	60106	Flying Fox	,,	,,	,,	—
4476	107	60107	Royal Lancer	,,	,,	,,	—
4477	108§	60108	Gay Crusader	,,	,,	,,	E
4478	109§	60109	Hermit	,,	,,	,,	—
4479	110	60110	Robert the Devil	,,	,,	,,	—
4480	111	60111	Enterprise	,,	,,	,,	G
4481	112§	60112	St. Simon	,,	,,	,,	—
2543	44	60044	Melton	,,	1924	,,	—
2544	45	60045	Lemberg	,,	,,	,,	H
2545	46	60046	Diamond Jubilee	,,	,,	,,	—
2546	47	60047	Donovan	,,	,,	,,	—
2547	48	60048	Doncaster	,,	,,	,,	—
2548	49§	60049	Galtee More	,,	,,	,,	—
2549	50§	60050	Persimmon	,,	,,	,,	—
2550	51	60051	Blink Bonny	,,	,,	,,	—
2551	52§	60052	Prince Palatine	,,	,,	,,	—
2552	53§	60053	Sansovino	,,	,,	,,	—
2553	54§	60054	Prince of Wales	,,	,,	,,	—
2554	55	60055	Woolwinder	,,	,,	,,	—
2555	56	60056	Centenary	,,	1925	,,	—
2556	57	60057	Ormonde	,,	,,	,,	—
2557	58	60058	Blair Athol	,,	,,	,,	—
2558	59	60059	Tracery	,,	,,	,,	—
2559	60§	60060	The Tetrarch	,,	,,	,,	—
2560	61	60061	Pretty Polly	,,	,,	,,	—
2561	62	60062	Minoru	,,	,,	,,	—
2562	63§	60063	Isinglass	,,	,,	,,	
2563	64	60064	(William Whitelaw) Tagalie	,,	1924	,,	K
2564	65	60065	Knight of Thistle	,,	,,	,,	K
2565	66	60066	Merry Hampton	,,	,,	,,	K

THE GRESLEY PACIFICS OF THE L.N.E.R.

L.N.E.R. Origi-nal No.	Thomp-son Renum-bering	British Railways No.	Name*	Ori-ginal Class	Date of Build-ing	Pres-ent Class	Notes
2566	67	60067	Ladas	A1	1924	A3	K
2567	68	60068	Sir Visto	,,	,,	,,	KN
2568	69§	60069	Sceptre	,,	,,	,,	K
2569	70§	60070	Gladiateur	,,	,,	,,	K
2570	71	60071	Tranquil	,,	,,	,,	K
2571	72	60072	Sunstar	,,	,,	,,	K
2572	73	60073	St. Gatien	,,	,,	,,	K
2573	74§	60074	Harvester	,,	,,	,,	GK
2574	75	60075	St. Frusquin	,,	,,	,,	K
2575	76	60076	Galopin	,,	,,	,,	K
2576	77§	60077	The White Knight	,,	,,	,,	KM
2577	78	60078	Night Hawk	,,	,,	,,	K
2578	79	60079	Bayardo	,,	,,	,,	GK
2579	80	60080	Dick Turpin	,,	,,	,,	K
2580	81	60081	Shotover	,,	,,	,,	GKM
2581	82	60082	Neil Gow	,,	,,	,,	K
2582	83	60083	Sir Hugo	,,	,,	,,	K
2743	89	60089	Felstead	A3	1928	,,	—
2744	90	60090	Grand Parade	,,	,,	,,	X
2745	91	60091	Captain Cuttle	,,	,,	,,	—
2746	92	60092	Fairway	,,	,,	,,	—
2747	93	60093	Coronach	,,	,,	,,	U
2748	94	60094	Colorado	,,	,,	,,	—
2749	95§	60095	Flamingo	,,	1929	,,	—
2750	96	60096	Papyrus	,,	,,	,,	Q
2751	97	60097	Humorist	,,	,,	,,	V
2752	98§	60098	Spion Kop	,,	,,	,,	—
2595	84	60084	Trigo	,,	1930	,,	—
2596	85	60085	Manna	,,	,,	,,	—
2597	86	60086	Gainsborough	,,	,,	,,	—
2598	87§	60087	(Rock Sand) Blenheim	,,	,,	,,	—
2599	88	60088	Book Law	,,	,,	,,	—
2795	99	60099	Call Boy	,,	,,	,,	—
2796	100	60100	Spearmint	,,	,,	,,	—
2797	101	60101	Cicero	,,	,,	,,	—
2500	35§	60035	Windsor Lad	,,	1934	,,	O
2501	36	60036	Colombo	,,	,,	,,	—
2502	37	60037	Hyperion	,,	,,	,,	—
2503	38	60038	Firdaussi	,,	,,	,,	—
2504	39	60039	Sandwich	,,	,,	,,	—
2505	40§	60040	Cameronian	,,	,,	,,	—
2506	41	60041	Salmon Trout	,,	,,	,,	—
2507	42	60042	Singapore	,,	,,	,,	—
2508	43	60043	Brown Jack	,,	1935	,,	—
2509	14	60014	Silver Link	A4	,,	A4	†RW
2510	15	60015	Quicksilver	,,	,,	,,	R

For Key to Notes, see page 122.

L.N.E.R. Origi- nal No.	Thomp- son Renum- bering	British Railways No.	Name*	Ori- ginal Class	Date of Build- ing	Pres- ent Class	Notes
2511	16	60016	*Silver King*	A4	1935	A4	R
2512	17	60017	*Silver Fox*	,,	,,	,,	R
4482	23	60023	*Golden Eagle*	,,	1936	,,	—
4483	24§	60024	*Kingfisher*	,,	,,	,,	—
4484	25§	60025	*Falcon*	,,	1937	,,	—
4485	26§	60026	*(Kestrel) Miles Beevor*	,,	,,	,,	—
4486	27§	60027	*Merlin*	,,	,,	,,	—
4487	28	60028	*(Sea Eagle) Walter K. Whigham*	,,	,,	,,	—
4488	9	60009	*(Osprey) Union of South Africa*	,,	,,	,,	S
4489	10	60010	*(Woodcock) Dominion of Canada*	,,	,,	,, ·	SZ
4490	11	60011	*Empire of India*	,,	,,	,,	S
4491	12	60012	*Commonwealth of Australia*	,,	,,	,,	SW
4492	13	60013	*Dominion of New Zealand*	,,	,,	,,	S
4493	29	60029	*Woodcock*	,,	,,	,,	—
4494	3	60003	*(Osprey) Andrew K. McCosh*	,,	,,	,,	W
4495	30	60030	*(Great Snipe) Golden Fleece*	,,	,,	,,	T
4496	8	60008	*(Golden Shuttle) Dwight D. Eisenhower*	,,	,,	,,	T
4497	31	60031	*Golden Plover*	,,	,,	,,	W
4498	7	60007	*Sir Nigel Gresley*	,,	,,	,,	—
4462	4	60004	*(Great Snipe) William Whitelaw*	,,	,,	,,	—
4463	18	60018	*Sparrow Hawk*	,,	,,	,,	—
4464	19	60019	*Bittern*	,,	,,	,,	—
4465	20	60020	*Guillemot*	,,	,,	,,	—
4466	6§	60006	*(Herring Gull) Sir Ralph Wedgwood*	,,	1938	,,	—
4467	21	60021	*Wild Swan*	,,	,,	,,	—
4468	22	60022	*Mallard*	,,	,,	,,	‡VF
4469	—	—	*(Gadwall) Sir Ralph Wedg- wood*	,,	,,	,,	Y
4499	2	60002	*(Pochard) Sir Murrough Wilson*	,,	,,	,,	—
4500	1	60001	*(Garganey) Sir Ronald Matthews*	,,	,,	,,	—
4900	32	60032	*Gannet*	,,	,,	,,	—
4901	5	60005	*(Capercaillie) Sir Charles Newton*	,,	,,	,,	V
4902	33	60033	*Seagull*	,,	,,	,,	VF
4903	34	60034	*(Peregrine) Lord Faringdon*	,,	,,	,,	VF

For Key to Notes, see Page 122.

THE GRESLEY PACIFICS OF THE L.N.E.R.

NOTES : * Names in brackets are original names of engines subsequently renamed.
† Ran 43 miles at 100 m.p.h. and touched 112½ m.p.h., September 27th, 1935. ‡ Attained
126 m.p.h., July 7th, 1938. A: Completely rebuilt in 1945 by Mr. E. Thompson with 3
independent sets of Walschaerts valve-motion, banjo dome, double exhaust and 250 lb.
pressure. B: First Gresley Pacific to work a 610-ton passenger train, September 3rd,
1922. C: Exhibited at British Empire Exhibition, Wembley, 1924. D: Worked
between Paddington and Plymouth, G.W.R., in the exchange tests, April-May, 1925.
E: First Pacific to have completely redesigned valve-motion for short cut-off working,
1925. F: Took part in Locomotive Exchange Trials over L.M., W. and S. Regions, summer
of 1948. G: Rebuilt with 220 lb. boiler and 43-element superheater, 1927. H: Rebuilt
as "G" and with cylinders lined up to 18½ in. diameter, 1927. K: Built by the North
British Locomotive Company. L: Fitted temporarily with 62-element superheater,
1926. M: Fitted with A.C.F.I. feed-water heaters and feed-pumps, 1929. N: Last
original "A1" Pacific to be converted to "A3," 1949. O: First "A3" Pacific to be
fitted with banjo dome for steam collection, 1934. P: Locomotive used on the
London—Leeds high speed test, November 30th, 1934, and first Gresley Pacific to
attain 100 m.p.h. Q: Locomotive used on the London—Newcastle high speed test,
March 5th, 1935; maximum speed 108 m.p.h. R: Assigned to the "Silver Jubilee"
streamline workings and at first painted grey. S: Assigned to the "Coronation"
streamline workings. T: Assigned to the "West Riding Limited" streamline workings.
U: Used for experiments in smoke deflection in 1932. V: Fitted with smoke deflectors,
double blast-pipe and double chimney. W: Middle cylinder lined up to 17 in. diameter,
1948. X: Severely damaged in Castlecary collision, December 10th, 1937; practically a
new engine, 1938. Y: Damaged beyond repair by a German bomb at York, April 29th,
1942, and subsequently scrapped. Z: Carries on smokebox bell presented by the
Canadian National Railways. §: For a brief period about 1947, before the Thompson
renumbering scheme came into force, the following Gresley Pacifics carried the temporary
numbers shown in brackets:—4472 (502), 4477 (507), 4478 (508), 4481 (511), 2548 (517),
2549 (518), 2551 (520), 2552 (521), 2553 (522), 2559 (528), 2562 (531), 2568 (537), 2569 (538),
2573 (542), 2576 (545), 2749 (558), 2752 (561), 2598 (565), 2500 (570), 2505 (575), 4483 (585),
4484 (586), 4485 (587), 4486 (588), and 4466 (605), 25 engines in all.

Appendix II

LEADING DIMENSIONS OF GRESLEY PACIFICS

Class	"A1"	"A3"	"A4"
Cylinders (3) diameter	20 in.	19 in.	18½ in.
„ stroke	26 in.	26 in.	26 in.
Coupled wheels, diameter	6 ft. 8 in.	6 ft. 8 in.	6 ft. 8 in.
Heating surface, tubes	2,715 sq. ft.	2,477 sq. ft.	2,345 sq. ft.
„ „ firebox	215 sq. ft.	215 sq. ft.	231 sq. ft.
„ „ total	2,930 sq. ft.	2,692 sq. ft.	2,576 sq. ft.
Superheating surface	525 sq. ft.	706 sq. ft.	750 sq. ft.
Firegrate area	41·25 sq. ft.	41·25 sq. ft.	41·25 sq. ft.
Working pressure, per sq. in.	180 lb.	220 lb.	250 lb.
Tractive effort (at 85% b.p.)	29,835 lb.	32,910 lb.	35,455 lb.
Adhesion weight	60·00 tons	66·15 tons	66·00 tons
Total engine weight (wkg. order)	92·45 tons	96·25 tons	102·95 tons
Tender coal capacity	9 tons	9 tons	9 tons
„ water „	5,000 gal.	5,000 gal.	5,000 gal.
„ weight (working order)	56·30 tons	56·30 tons	*64·95 tons
Engine & tender weight	148·75 tons	152·55 tons	*167·90tons

* Corridor tender.

NOTE: *Above are the latest official figures, and differ in minor details from certain of the figures
on the engine diagrams on pp. 126 to 128, which were compiled at an earlier date.*

Appendix III

DIAGRAMS OF
LOCOMOTIVES AND LOCOMOTIVE FOOTPLATES

"A3" PACIFIC CAB

(Rebuilt "A10" with right-hand drive)

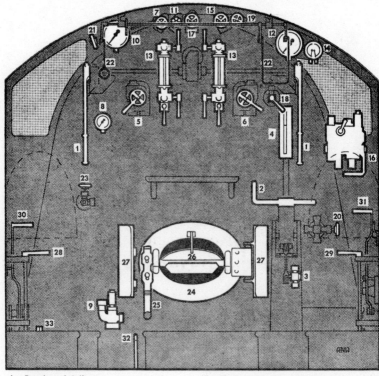

1.	Regulator handle.
2.	Reversing gear handle.
3.	Reversing gear locking valve.
4.	Cut-off indicator.
5.	Exhaust steam injector, combined steam supply and clack valve.
6.	Live steam injector, combined steam supply and clack valve.
7.	Steam heating supply valve.
8.	Steam heating pressure gauge.
9.	Steam heating pressure relief valve.
10.	Boiler steam pressure gauge.
11.	Boiler steam pressure gauge cut-off valve.
12.	Steam chest pressure gauge.
13.	Water level gauge.
14.	Vacuum brake gauge.
15.	Ejector steam supply valve.
16.	Ejector and brake application lever.
17.	Blower steam supply valve.
18.	Blower valve.
19.	Steam sanding, steam supply valve.
20.	Steam sanding valve.
21.	Steam fountain cut-off valve.
22.	Whistle control.
23.	Coal slacking hose water valve.
24.	Fire door.
25.	Fire door bolt.
26.	Adjustable half-door.
27.	Fire screens.
28.	Exhaust steam injector water valve.
29.	Live steam injector water valve.
30.	Cylinder drain cocks lever.
31.	Sanding lever.
32.	Damper control.
33.	Key square operating drop grate.

APPENDIX III

"A4" PACIFIC CAB

(with left-hand drive.)

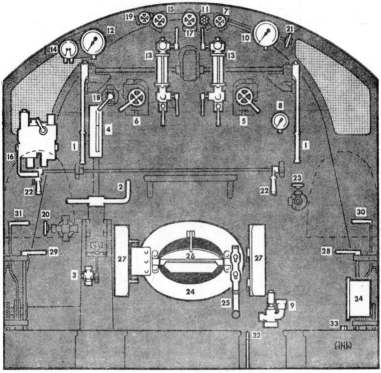

1. Regulator handle.	17. Blower steam supply valve.
2. Reversing gear handle.	18. Blower valve.
3. Reversing gear locking valve.	19. Steam sanding, steam supply valve.
4. Cut-off indicator.	20. Steam sanding valve.
5. Exhaust steam injector, combined steam supply and clack valve.	21. Steam fountain cut-off valve.
	22. Whistle control.
6. Live steam injector, combined steam supply and clack valve.	23. Coal slacking hose water valve.
	24. Fire door.
7. Steam heating supply valve.	25. Fire door bolt.
8. Steam heating pressure gauge.	26. Adjustable half-door.
9. Steam heating pressure relief valve.	27. Fire screens.
10. Boiler steam pressure gauge.	28. Exhaust steam injector water valve.
11. Boiler steam pressure gauge cut-off valve.	29. Live steam injector water valve.
12. Steam chest pressure gauge.	30. Cylinder drain cocks lever.
13. Water level gauge.	31. Sanding lever.
14. Vacuum brake gauge.	32. Damper control.
15. Ejector steam supply valve.	33. Key square operating drop grate.
16. Ejector and brake application lever.	34. Flaman speed recorder.

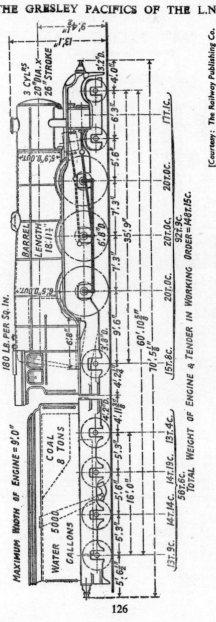

[Courtesy: The Railway Publishing Co.

DIAGRAM OF CLASS "A1" (LATER "A10") PACIFIC.

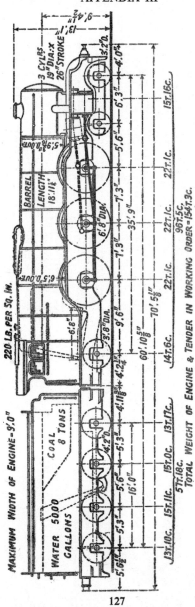

[Courtesy: The Railway Publishing Co.

DIAGRAM OF CLASS "A3" PACIFIC WITH BANJO DOME.

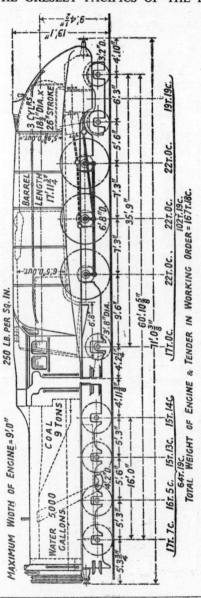

[Courtesy: The Railway Publishing Co.

DIAGRAM OF CLASS "A4" PACIFIC.